# CYBER
## HAND
# PUNK
## BOOK

[The Real Cyberpunk Fakebook]

# CYBERPUNK
## HANDBOOK

## [The Real Cyberpunk Fakebook]

## St. Jude, R.U. Sirius and Bart Nagel

ARROW

Published in the United Kingdom in 1996 by
Arrow Books

1 3 5 7 9 10 8 6 4 2

First published in the United Kingdom in 1996 by Arrow

Arrow Books Limited
Random House UK Ltd
20 Vauxhall Bridge Road, London, SW1V 2SA

Random House Australia (Pty) Limited
16 Dalmore Drive, Scoresby, Vic 3179

Random House New Zealand Limited
18 Poland Road, Glenfield
Auckland 10, New Zealand

Random House South Africa (Pty) Limited
PO Box 2263, Rosebank 2121, South Africa

Random House UK Limited Reg. No 954009

A CIP catalogue record for this book is available from the British Library

Papers used by Random House UK Limited are natural, recyclable products made from
wood grown in sustainable forests. The manufacturing processes conform to the
environmental regulations of the country of origin

Printed and bound in Great Britain by
BPC Consumer Books Ltd
A member of
The British Printing Company Ltd

ISBN 0 09 9791617

For my dear people, for the Cypherpunks, for Kevin Crow, Nesta Stubbs, The Omega, Phiber, and hackers everywhere, though none dare call it cyberpunk.

—St. Jude

I would like to acknowledge my father, Arnold Goffman (1922-1977) from whom I inherited an irreverence towards authority and an unrelenting sense of the ridiculous. Thanks, dad.

—R.U. Sirius

For Karen M. Huff, Marian Jansen op de Haar, Lynda Murphy, Barbara Roberts, Jeannine Cuevas, Hal Martin Fogel, Fred Dodsworth, and for my dwarf twin in a previous life; Kim Blake.

—Bart Nagel

# Foreword to The Real Cyberpunk Fakebook

*by Bruce Sterling, Renowned Cyberpunk Writer*

I like this book so much that I'm thinking of changing my name to St.Erling. You couldn't ask for better guides to faking cyberpunk than these utterly accomplished Bay Area fraudsters. These characters are such consummate boho hustlers that they make Aleister Crowley look like Rebecca of Sunnybrook Farm.

I don't believe in smart drugs, and I've never believed in smart drugs, but I do believe the following. It's genuinely useful to society to have some small, contained fraction of reckless fools who are willing to consume untested and unknown devices and substances. Sure, most of them will have their hearts explode or break out into great purple bleeding thalidomide warts. But who knows, maybe someday one of these jaspers will be eating handfuls of psychoactive crap out of some hippie pharmacy and he or she will suddenly learn to read Japanese in the original in six days. That's not at all likely, but it could happen—grant me the possibility.

The only drawback to this decentralized, libertarian, free-market regime of biomedical research is that you have to be ruthlessly prepared to sacrifice certain people—just write 'em off, basically, like a cageful of control hamsters down at the NIMH. And if I ever met a man uniquely suited to this particular cutting-edge role in life, it is R.U. Sirius. R. U. Sirius basically resembles Gomez Addams in a purple fedora with an Andy Warhol badge pinned to the brim. The moment I met R.U., I felt a strong need to pith him and examine his viscera. I'm sure there are many other free-lance biomedical researchers who will feel the same intellectual impulse. Read this book and you'll see what I mean.

Then there's this saint person. Never draw to an inside straight. Never eat at a place called Mom's. And never eat a bag of ephedrine and a pumpkin pie ("the *whip* of vegetables!") from a California blonde who doesn't even have a real name. This female personage is so appallingly cagey that even her main squeeze delights in cryptographically baffling the NSA. If Pat Buchanan ever gets his not-so-secret wish and sets up a domestic American gulag for counterculture thought-criminals, the Judester's gonna be way, *way* up on the list—maybe even number two, right after Bob Dobbs. Her trial's likely to prove rather interesting, however, as she only commits "crimes" in areas of social activity that haven't even been defined yet, much less successfully crim-inalized. A serious legal study of this woman's spectrum of activities would be like a CAT-scan of the American unconscious.

There's also Bart Nagel, who is too nice a guy to be in the company of these people.

Almost everything in this swell book is completely true. Except for everything about me. And my closest co-conspirators. We actual cyberpunks—by this I mean *science fiction writers*, dammit, the people for whom the c-word was invented, the people who were professionally ahead of our time and were cyberpunks *twelve years ago*—we never sneer and we never dress like, God forbid, Tom Wolfe. We just laugh at inappropriate times (like when testifying in Congress) and we dress and act just like industrial design professors.

I hope this brief intro clears up any confusion. If you have any trouble at all with this book, take full advantage of your online d00dship and send email. Don't be afraid to ask "stupid" questions—that's what the Internet is for! Ask nice, big, broad, open-ended questions. Stuff like "I'm doing a term paper so please tell me everything you know about cyberspace" or "I'm cyberpunk fan from Bulgaria and Enlgish not too good, but please say more what is about Virtual Reality?"

Just don't send the email to me, of course. Send email to *them*. After this book, they deserve it! I feel sure that you'll get prompt answers that will surprise you.

# The
# Authors
# Explain
## *A Technical Guide to This Technical Guide*

### Words in Boldface

These are terms that are defined in **Building Your Cyber Word Power**. Check there for anything that baffles you. Sometimes there's a boldface word in the dictionary that refers to a chapter subheading, and then you must practice your **haqr smarts** in order to find it. If all else fails, you could ask Bruce Sterling at his secret email address— bruces@well.com. He will know.

### The Shuriken Awards

We may sometimes succumb to the temptation to rate things the way snotty critics do, by awarding stars. However, we will award *shuriken*, a cyber kinda star:

A shuriken is a throwing star—a shiny-steel, sharp-edged, sharp-pointed weapon from Japan (which is cyberpunk's original home in certain misty urban legends). The shuriken itself as an assault weapon would rate one-half shuriken on a scale of four. A hydrogen bomb would rate five shuriken. You get the idea.

Occasionally we may add propeller beanies to the shuriken.

This indicates **nerd**ly interest over and above a cyberpunk rating. Propeller head is an ancient term for nerd. The real name for that key on the Macintosh is not COM-MAND, but PROPELLER, and this is why.

# tents

# ntents

Co

CENSORED

# Conten

# [ CYBERPUNK... WHY??  OKAY... HOW?? ]

# Chapter 1
# Cyberpunk:
# A Challenging
# Postmodern Lifestyle!
## *Why Bother? Big Wins! (And Unexpected Smallstuff)*

Cyberpunk is extremely hip. Being extremely hip is the last hope for people with no money and no power. Being hip gets you big wins in the status game. Hipness can crush your enemies and attract the apposite sex. Best of all, cyberpunk is the next big thing AFTER the next big thing. You can hop on the cyberpunk bandwagon and coast for a long, long time. Think of the money you'll save on wardrobe updates! The worry you'll save on lifestyle decisions!

Cyberpunk has not yet been co-opted. In fact, this handbook is the very first exploitation of this hip new underground trend. This is the ground floor. Get in on it!

# Chapter 2
# Achieving Cyberpunk
*Being It or Faking It*

What is there to know about being a cyberpunk? Leather jacket, mirrorshades—that just about does it, right? This kind of patronizing shirt must farking DIE.*

You think cyberpunk is just a leather jacket, some chrome studs, and fully reflective sunglasses? You think that's all there is? Hah! You can find those on Kansas City bikers and the whole California Highway Patrol. The true cyberpunk might tuck a *cellular-modem laptop* under a spiked leather arm, and a *laser pointer* in the upper zip pocket. Or, a true cyberpunk may look just like YOU. But sHe** who knows doesn't tell, and **hirm who tells doesn't know.

\* Since we can't afford to offend any parental units who might purchase this book for their family circle, all chancy verbs and nouns have been cleverly encyphered. This is in the spirit of true cyberpunk-hood, see **Encryption**.

\*\* All pronouns in this book started life as intact males—he, his, and him. If anything bad happened to them afterwards, blame the Riot Grrrlz Bobbitt Squad.

The lifestyle and goals of the true cyberpunk are carefully guarded secrets in a life *totally devoted* to coolness and secrecy. We will PIERCE THE VEIL, and REVEAL those SECRETS. We will display for you the INNER CYBERPUNK. We will give you everything you need to know about embarking on this challenging lifestyle. When you have read to the end of this EASY handbook, if you DON'T pass the hipness quiz… well, just read it again. But turn your TV up louder.

# Chapter 3
# A Style Guide to
# the Cybertypes
*Recognizing Them
and Fitting In*

While a cyberpunk is commonly a middleclass white male with way too many electrons, there are varieties of cyberpunk. Underlying all the types and genres is Basic Cyber Style, which breaks down to physical gear and mental attitude:

**Basic Cyberpunk Gear** is simple. Black leather jacket. Boots. Mirrorshades. Laser pointer. (We don't know why all cyberpunks need a laser pointer, but it's mandatory.) We'll give you a more elaborate guide to basic cyberpunk gear. Later.

**The Basic Cyberpunk Attitude** is quiet assurance. Subdued swashbuckling. Maybe a little menace.

With these cyberpunk basics you can navigate through

all the sub-genres. But if you want to pass as a native in a particular cyber sub-scene without getting jeered at or beaten up, you gotta accessorize, and pay close attention to detail.

**Motorpsycho Maniacs**
Cyberbikers pack the mystique of both worlds—high tech, and big loud greasy engines. Standard cyberpunk costume is ideal for riding motorcycles, and a mirror-shades helmet is a big plus for the cyber look—mega robotic coolness. Motorcycles are dangerous and can kill you. This is also cool.

**Goths, Deathcore, and Vampire-Wannabes**
Ideally, for this sub-scene, you should know about The Cure, which is a band. To fit in, grow your hair big and dye it blue-black. Spray it with **Aquanet White** to make it stick out, medusa-like. Go to a kidshop and buy plastic fangs. (The kind that glow in the dark are funny. Funny is NOT the object here.) All sexes should wear a Victorian shirt-blouse —white or black only—that gapes to show flesh. You must practice looking tormented, tall and thin. The ideal is chalk-

white face makeup with blueblack eyesockets. Blueblack makeup with white eyesockets is untested, but might work very well, if you avoid a minstrel look. At all times think intensity and torment. Torment… and ironic bitterness. No giggling or snickering, no kidding.

## Riot Grrrls

These are fierce girls who like tech. This is a sexist category, but there we are: girls only. A grrrl can be called "d00d" and "guy" at all times, but a non-female guy is not a grrrl. This is just the way things are.

If you're a grrrl, you can wear anything you want to, because you're there to defend it. This is true for anybody, really—look as tough as you wanta be, and be ready to back it up. Fierce is good. Grrrls with tech expertise are irresistible. NOTHING is more attractive than a fierce, blazing, ninja-type grrrl right now, and if she knows UNIX or phone-freeking, the world is hers. Hrrrs.

## Technopagans/Ravers/Neohippies

Don't worry about this one. This scene is free, loving, noncomforming, spontaneous. You can dress any old way and fit right in...

*Unless you don't look cool.*

Maybe you should stick to basic cyberpunk. Dancing in leather is hot as h*ck, but sweating is better than not looking cool. Non-cyber ravers favor floppy hats, five kinds of plaid 'n' paisley, and multiple organ piercings. They sometimes take raver drugs. These drugs make you fonder of other people than you really want to be. (The morning-after Revulsion attacks can be nasty.) In this scene, pretending to be on raver drugs is recommended, and easy, too. Unfocus your eyes and smile lovingly. In black leather you won't have to worry so much about getting hugged.

## Academic Cyber-Wannabes

Students, teachers, whatever, dress down. Like you're always en route to a garage sale... maybe to donate what you're wearing. *Casual.* Jeans, black leather jacket, laser pointer. No tweed, notice, and no Birkenstocken. If you flash paperbacks by the Krokers, Paul Virilio and Jean Baudrillard, it means you're serious. Paperbacks by Mark Leyner and Kathy Acker means you're *way past* serious.

## Cybercowboys/grrrls

Some of these people come from Texas or Oklahoma. In this crew, to yer cyberbasics you add a cowboy hat, cowboy boots, and grow any hair you've got really *long*. Males should try to get hair somewhere on their faces.

## Science Fiction Writers

Full-steam straight-ahead hard edge, with a permanent sneer. Just to twist heads, some male writers go for the Tom Wolfe effete look—blue blazer and wing-tips. Still they sneer.

William Gibson

## Web Crawlers and Other Bourgeois Types

You don't really care about this one, do you? You do? Subscribe to *Wired*. Next.

## Deep Geek: Supernerds,
## Hackers, Wizards, Phone Phreakers

Things get difficult here. Deep geekware is unstandard. Very heavy Wizards can look like accountants, or like streetpeople. Facial hair and Goodwill Casual happen a lot. Chubby happens too, since these guys don't do enough dancing in leather pants. To get along in this scene, you

really need to be very smart, very funny, or very sexy. To work yourself up to smart at least, learn UNIX. Or carry the *2600* zine in your back pocket and read that. Practice being technical. But until you get good, wear your cyber-basics and never leave home without your laser pointer. This will draw the admiration of people who don't know any better, which has its own rewards. Leading us inevitably to the final category…

### Phonies, Poseurs and Pretenders (Taking the Easy Way In)

Don't think: scheme! Forget about reading books, buy no computers or widgets. Don't do or buy *anything*. Save all your money for clothes and art materials. Make your girl/boyfriend help you assemble your hi-tek *models*—you're gonna need mockups of a laptop computer, a personal communicator, a beep-er, maybe even a fake stun-gun. Realism is the key. Then wear them all with *attitude*. You're better than real. Strut. Sneer. Remember the 3 disses: distrust, disrespect, distroy. Wait, that's not right, is it?

**photo of Billy Idol goes here**

We know there are going to be mutterings about this category. Grum-blings that being a poseur is not as easy as we think. A poseur has a lot of overhead—in worry, just for starts—what if you're exposed as **a clueless**? And having to stay locked to the HOTWIRED Website to catch what you should be imitating? Dang!

# SECTION 2

SECTION II: CYBERPUNK...

## [ CYBERPUNK... KNOWING ABOUT IT! ]

# Chapter 4
# Building Your Cyber Word Power

## Part 1: *A Dictionary of Terminally Hip Jargon and Useful Expressions*

**acronym**: A word made from the initials of a name or phrase. Such as TLA. Three-Letter Acronym. Right.

**AFAIK**: As far as I know. An **acronym**, in **haqrese**.

**AI**: Artificial Intelligence. The next best thing to real.

**aka**: Also known as. An acronym coined by the FBI in its popular Most Wanted lists.

**alliance**: Among **phreaker**s, a former AT&T trademark which refers to teleconferencing systems.

**anarchist**: Somebody who feels that governments are an unreasonable restraint on free humans' being.

**anarcho-cryptographer**: An anarchist who hopes to bring down the established order by persuading everybody to use **encryption**.

**anonymity**: There's no handle like *no* handle. Being completely unknown means you can't be traced. Maybe. You can be anonymous online by bouncing your email or postings through **remailers**. Who are you? Only penet.fi knows for sure.

**Aquanet White**: This is the most intense hairspray on the planet, for that BIG **goth** hair. Since you're being so attentive, here's a bonus goth haiku:

Sun! Hide white skin, run—

Burning, cloaked, I run... day sky!...

Must... find... Aquanet

**ASCII**: An **acronym** for… well, nobody remembers what it's an acronym for, but it means just plain keyboard characters, like your **dot.sig** is made of.  This is a portrait of R.U. Sirius rendered in ASCII art:

```
##############
#   /==$=\ )  #
#  // -00 (\  #
#  ((( — )))  #
# ))))\ /(((( #
##############
```

So he comes out looking something like the cartoon character Cathy—yeah, but that's the nature of the medium. St.Jude would look exactly the same, only no hat.  Being subtle or elegant in ASCII is a real challenge.

**attitude**:  Strutting.  Sneering.  Being BAD.  Attitude is what all primates do to make their enemies feel inadequate.  Keep it in mind.

**bah**:  Expresses the whole range of haqr negative emotions, from dysgruntlement up through horrible contempt, as in response to **lameness**.

**bahaha**:  A haqr evil laugh.  Other common evil laughs are NYaa-hahah and pchtkwaaahahahaha.

**bang**:  Old haqr term for exclamation point.  Sometimes bangs are a series of characters to add emphasis: w00t@%$%$@!

**BBS**:  A computerized bulletin-board system.  Imagine a bulletin board in the sky.  It's subdivided into sections by topic. The cards displayed under each topic are email postings. You read them to follow the conversations. You can add your own comments or rebuttals. Some boards have a chat area where you can talk real-time, sort of like ham radio. The underground BBS chat areas are hangout places where bored hacker/phreaker types exchange quips and insults. Good H/P boards have libraries of up-to-date info on tools of the trade.

**beta release, in beta test**: Not ready for prime time. This comes from the beta phase of program testing, when bugs are collected from patient users up for major **lossage**. "In beta" can describe anything unpleasing or forked up. If it's really **FUBARed**, it can be called *alpha*-release, which is software still being tested in-house, by programmers and unlucky affiliates.

**Big Room, The**: Used to refer to the place you went OUT to, with one big bright light up there or else many small ones, you know? Now means the place you go INTO, the new Big Room—Cyberspace.

**bogus**: Untrue. Unreal. A spoof. Also, **bogosity**, which is the state of being bogus, and **bogon**, a unit of bogosity. Then there's the **bogometer**…

**boho**:  Bohemian.  Means like, counter-cultural.  Underground.  Alternative, with people in black clothes.

**boxing**:  Using a gadget to get free phone calls.  The Red Box plays the tones of coins registering in a pay phone.  The Rainbow Box incorporates many previous boxes in one diabolical widget, thanks to our Dutch buddies.

**bridge**:  A **hack** into the phone company itself, allowing multiple **phreaker**s to cross-talk, like a high-tech, illegal party line.  Appropriating the phone company's own **PBX** systems is considered good **phun**.

**btw**:  By the way, in **hackerese**.

**carding**:  Making purchases on a phony or stolen credit account.  The card as a physical chunk of plastic has become more or less irrelevant.

**celibate**: Non-hacking hacker.  Some times this is a haqr who has been **newtered**.

**clueless, a**:  (by analogy from "a homeless"??)  One who doesn't get it and is doomed.

**codez**: Phone numbers and authorization codes that allow you to make phree fonecalls.

**codez kid**: A person whose purpose in life is finding ways to make phree fone calls. This is a terrible thing to call someone. Much worse than **punk**.

**coldlist:** Shortlist for oblivion. By analogy to hotlist.

**Con:** Convention, or maybe it was Conference—nobody cares any more. A Con is a gathering of haqrz. There are several every year. The most famous is Hacking at the End of the Universe, held by the former Hac-tic in Amsterdam. Next is Hacking On Planet Earth, HOPE, and two infamous Cons are in Austin TX—SummerCon, in the summer, and HoHoCon, figure it out.

**cookbook guyz**: Haqr wannabes who don't figure out how to do things for themselves. They copy down procedures for hacking computers or fones and follow the instructions, like using a cookbook. Everybody has to start out this way. Get over it.

**cracker, kraqr**: Somebody who breaks the copy protection on computer games or intrudes into other people's computers. Or invades cyberspace in strange ways. Or pirates any of the media. See **pirating** and **hack** and **spoof**.

**cryonics**: Freezing your body (or just your head, on the budget plan) so that you can be revived (or provided with a whole-body transplant) at some time in the future when
1. They can do that sort of thing, and
2. They really WANT to do that sort of thing for frozen heads like you. See **futurespoofing**.

**cryptography, cryptology**: Cryptology is the study of **encryption**. Cryptography is *doing* it. See **public key encryption** for a full rundown.

**culture hacker**: A pirate whose raw material is the society itself. A **détournement** specialist, who drives the **memes** of the culture on wild detours.

**cyberspace**: The planetary Net linked by phonelines and satellites, whose nodes are computers and human beings. An online metaverse that's now realler than what's outside your window.

**cyberpunk**: 1. A citizen of cyberspace. 2. A citizen of cyberspace who wears mirrorshades indoors, at night.

**cyber-yup**: A tourist on the info highway. A **Net-crawler**, a Web Browser. If artists and nerds are sort of squatting or homesteading their homepages, cyber-yups create theirs as investment property.

**cypherpunk**: A guerrilla in the war for privacy and lots more **encryption**.

**cypherpunks**: A **list** of people interested in cryptology and cryptography.

**darqside**: Antisocial. Evil. Weird. Someone who dares things you wouldn't, or couldn't.

**data**: This is supposed to be plural. These data. If you don't wanna deal with that, see **information**.

**cyberpunk**: 1. A citizen of cyberspace. 2. A citizen of cyberspace who wears mirrorshades indoors, at night.

**deck**: What cyberpunks in *Neuromancer* typed on and jacked in through… like a keyboard with phonejacks that plug into YOU.

**deep geek**: For the specs on deep geek, see Chapter Three.

**defect**: Roll over to the **narqside**.

**détournement**: Cultural hijacking. Taking something that has a usual meaning and making it play your way. A détournement is a cultural **hack**.

**dharma combat**: Wrangling over standards and protocols, as in the **IETF**. *Dharma* is Buddhist for the operating rules of the universe. Lots of **deep geek**s are Buddhists, Buddhist-wannabes, or jack-Buddhists.

**digital cash**: The Philosopher's Stone of the Nineties. Or maybe the Brooklyn Bridge. And good luck with it.

**diy**: Do it yourself. A part of **haqr mind,** see Chapter Eight.

**domain name**: This is part of the eddress that humans use. If you subscribe to an online service, like US Online, your domain eddress is theirs. Your whole eddress is whatever your handle is—say skulldrool— plus the server's domain name, like so: skulldrool@usol.com. Top level domain names are countries, like .au for australia, or categories, like .com, for company, .org for organization, .gov for the government, .mil for the military, etc. Domain names can be bought, and maybe they can be hacked. For example, if I had a military-industrial complex, I might hack an eddress like dark.satanic.mil.

**dot.plan**: This is a file in your home directory within UNIX that people can read when they **finger** you. Your dot.plan file (actually it's just .plan) is where you put your advertisements for yourself. A typical dot.plan might start with a motto or a fave quote, such as, "In theory, there's no difference between theory and practice. But in practice, there is." Followed by as intriguing and flattering a profile of yourself as you can whomp together.

**dot.sig**: This is your online signature, your digigraph, which you can tack onto the end of all your online appearances. A dot.sig is usually made up of thought-provoking quotes and **ASCII** graphics. While somebody has to **finger** you to get your **dot.plan**, everybody is forced to see your dot.sig every time they read your postings or get email from you. Think of your dot.sig as a billboard advertising yourself.

**eddress**: **Email** address.

**e-lite**: (Pronounced "e-light.") A lightweight posing as **elite**.

**eLiTe, 3L1T3, eleet, 31337, 'l33t, etcetc**: Those haqrz who Know Everything There Is To Know, and too bad about you. The very best of these guys teach what they know to the less fortunate.

**elite po1ntz**: What the truly **elite** don't need to score.

**email**: Electronic mail, sent via your **modem**, over telephone wires, via other computers, to other people.

**emsg**: **Email** message.

**encryption**: Turning your incriminating email into innocent ones and zeroes. Making your naughty bits look like *random* bits. See **public key encryption** for the **diy** how-to**.**

**ezine**: An electronic magazine, distributed on the Net. Some ezines, such as *GeekGirl*, are also printed on paper, on real live dead trees.

**f2f**: Face-to-face, as when you **meat** someone **IRL**. Time spent f2f is called face time.

**fangs**: Store-bought teeth for hanging out in **goth** clubs. Subtle is good—aim for the merest glint of a fang from deep within shadows. Fangs must NOT glow in the dark.

**FAQ**: A list of Frequently Asked Questions, with answers. **FTP**ing the FAQ is how you orient yourself when you join a new conversation online. A FAQ will give you the background info you need in order to understand the ongoing postings on a **USENET** group or a **list**.

**finger**: This is a UNIX command that fetches you the **dot.plan** of a person you're curious about. You use it like this:
finger nostril@nose.org.

**flame**: To **taunt** or insult someone online.

**FTP, FSP**: FTP is File Transfer Protocol, if you still care about acronyms, and FSP—File Server Protocol—is the more anonymous version. FTP sites on the Internet are like supermarkets where you can browse for interesting stuff to download to your own computer.

**FUBARed**: Say "foo-barred." Hackerese for Forked Up Beyond All Recognition. As opposed to okay.

**futurehaqing**: Devilishly clever forecasting. Extra-sensory prediction.
*Free Bonus Futurehaq: Next year, having your own* **domain name** *will be BIG STATUS.*

**futurespoofing**: This is tech that is obviously the next thing after the current thing, but we're not really there, are we? It's tragic. We want it so bad, and it just doesn't work... yet. You're good to go with **cryonics** and the Personal Communicator? You're gonna put your money down for them? YOU WILL, maybe, but in the meantime YOU CAN'T.

**fyi**: For yr information. Common **hackerese acronym**.

**good hack**: See Chapter 17 for **What Cyberpunks Actually Admire, and Why**.

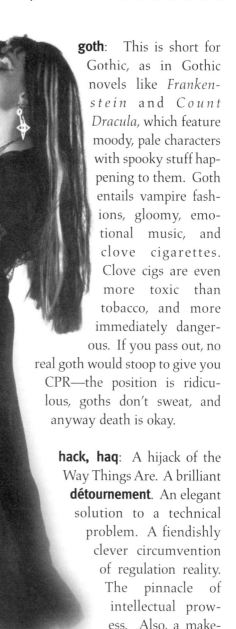

**goth**: This is short for Gothic, as in Gothic novels like *Franken-stein* and *Count Dracula*, which feature moody, pale characters with spooky stuff happening to them. Goth entails vampire fashions, gloomy, emotional music, and clove cigarettes. Clove cigs are even more toxic than tobacco, and more immediately dangerous. If you pass out, no real goth would stoop to give you CPR—the position is ridiculous, goths don't sweat, and anyway death is okay.

**hack, haq**: A hijack of the Way Things Are. A brilliant **détournement**. An elegant solution to a technical problem. A fiendishly clever circumvention of regulation reality. The pinnacle of intellectual prowess. Also, a makeshift solution.

**hack, hax, haxor**: To hack, the verb!  As in,
i am *l33t.* i hAX0rEd i-2600.com!

**hacker, haqr, haquer, haxor**:  1. A *ronin* (masterless
samurai) who swashbuckles through cyberspace battling
security systems in order to liberate imprisoned data.  2.
A criminal, dangerous to civil order and accountancy.  3.
A lonely, housebound 15-yr-old who wants to run free
through fields of pure information.

**hacker ethic**:  The hacker ethic is an ancient creed.  It
goes something like this.  Since information really longs
to be free, and since the quest for knowledge should not
be inhibited by passwords or protection schemes, it's
okay if you intrude, lurk, look—but don't touch.
Mature hackers have always worried about the kidz
with no ethics at all.  These kidz usually hit ethical
puberty.

**handle**: A pseudonym—an alternate identity—that you
use online.  Handles often express lots of **attitude**, like
Exterminator or Death Vegetable.  Handles make for a
shaky identity, though—there are *several* people known
as Count Zero.  You can sign your handle with a key (see
**public key encryption**) that makes your handle unique.
If enough people do this it could be the basis for a whole
new form of society.  Handles are a starting point for
freedom of expression.  (Somewhere a handle is waiting
for YOU.)

**haqr, haqrz**:  Usual way of spelling **hacker, hackers.**  A
recent and elegant variant:  haquer.  A new and punker-
ly version:  haxor.  They're all pronounced hacker.

**haqr smarts, haqrly attitude**: The mindset to take things apart and see how they work. Haqr smarts applies to everything you're faced with, **f2f** or online. The haqr mindset is like Bushido for the samurai, only you use yr brain instead of a katana. Are you following me here?

**haq-speak, hackerese, haqrese**: You might get the idea that this is a way to **hack** the whole communication process... and you'd be right.

First, haqrese has **acronym**s for common online expressions, like **btw**. These save typing, and maybe stave off for awhile the **RSI**.

Also, there are weird spellings to save keystrokes AND baffle **newbie**s. Ingenious spellings add color and dash, and if you really can't type—or spell—no one will ever know. For starters, interchange f and ph. And explode the limits of **ascii** by creating your own typefaces, like this:

| | | | | | |
|---:|:---:|:---|:---:|:---:|:---|
| /- | = | A | /\/\ | = | M |
| I> or I) | = | D | ]\I | = | N |
| 3 | = | E | zero | = | O |
| ]=[ | = | H | $ | = | S |
| 1 or ! | = | i | z | = | final S |
| q or ]< or X | = | K | + | = | t |
| 7 or I_ | = | L | \/\/ | = | W |

Y0U $H0UI_D ]\I0W B3 AB73 +0 R3AI) +H3z \/\/URI>z!

**heh:** Expresses the whole range of positive haqr emotions, from smugness up through nudge-wink to LOL, even unto ROFLMAO.

**homepage:** Your "place in the country" on the Web. Yes, a homepage is big status right now, but next year, marq my words, your newsdeliveryperson's cat will have a homepage, and big status will be having your own domain name on the Net. Fast.eddie.net? Yeah, that's coming, because the year after that... Look, if you worry about big status, you better subscribe to a lot of Silicon Valley venture-capital newsletters—right now, hear—and hire somebody to scour them for clues.

**hotlist:** Your little black book. Your list of hot Websites to loll around in... Also a verb, as in "Hotlist THAT one, baby!"

**HPCAV**: Acronym for Hack/Phreak/Card/Anarchy/Virus—areas of interest in the computer underground. Sometimes just H/P.

**HTML**: Hypertext Markup Language. The high-level formatting language that lets you create **homepage**s with **Hypertext**.

**HVAC**: Heating, Ventilation, Air Conditioning.

**Hypertext**: The land of the living footnotes. In the Web, Hypertext contains highlighted words that represent **URL**s. When you click on an active word you hop to that URL—actually, your Net program connects to that URL and >pop!< there you are, in that word's contextual text environment.  If this here that you're reading were a Hypertext you would be able to click on a word such as **Hyp-hop** and instantly you would

**Hyp-hop**:  Skip along through the Hypertext.

**IETF**:  The Internet Engineering Taskforce.  The ad-hoc body of **deep geek**s that imagine the Internet into exis- tence, via **RFC**s, helpful comments, and **dharma combat**.

**ILF**:  The Information Liberation Front.  ("Information Longs to be Free.")  The ILF is sort of like Amnesty Inter- national for **data**, but with lower overhead.  Originally just a joke within **cypherpunks**, the imaginary ILF now gets the credit when haqrs post copyrighted or secret information.—"This special report brought to you by the Information Liberation Front!"  ILF is also used as a verb, as in "We were thinking of ILFing the original Pen- tium specs."

**IMO, IMHO**:  In my [humble?] opinion.  **Haq-speak**.

**information**:  The real currency of the world.  Money is valuable only because it can be exchanged for this.

**IRC**:  Internet relay chat.  A club in cyberspace where you can hang out and typetalk real-time with others (yes, by typing on a keyboard over a **modem** on a phone wire).

**IRL**:  In real life.  Sorta derogatory, as in **meat** someone **f2f**, **IRL**.  Implies that online is better.  Realer.  Hmm.

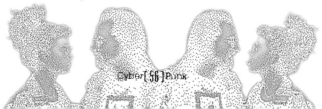

**k-**:  A prefix to anything.  K= kilo, one thousand.  Very, major, extremely.  In the early eighties a warez-guy, AppleBandit, had a keyboard that stuttered, producing **k-kool**.  Kidz on his Safehouse BBS thought it meant something.

**k**:  Extremely cool.  Dreamed up by Swamp Rat & GA Ellsworth, as in, "That is *so k!*"

**k-kool, k-kewl**:  k + cool.  Cool, however you spell it, can't be defined here in one sentence.  What do you think this whole book's about?

**k-lamer, k-loser**:  An ultimately inept, primitive person with a low level of technical know-how, **a clueless**.

**kludge**:   A programmer's jerry-rigged makeshift thing that may last for decades.  See **UNIX**.

**k-rad**:  k + radical.  Daring, masterly, inventive.  Alternate definition:  "A thousand points of rad."  (Made up by one of the Counts Zero.)

**lagged**:  Behind time, slow to hear things, out of the loop.  Or outright retarded.  "You say that, you're either lagged or lagged in your head."

**lame, lamer, lameness**:   Inept, ill-thought-out, **rancid**. Unworthy—"This guy's a total lamer!  He doesn't know that ALL BSD-derived kernels are subject to the sequence number attack!"

**list, mailing list**:  Something like an interactive online magazine.  You can send a posting to a list if you know its eddress, but you can receive postings only if you subscribe to it.  You can sometimes subscribe to a list by emailing the majordomo program at its eddress—

To:  majordomo@eddress.com
Subject: SUBSCRIBE listname

Just to be sure, put the "SUBSCRIBE listname" request in the body of the message, too.  Majordomo will add your eddress to its mailing list, send you a welcome note, instructions for unsubscribing, and maybe a **FAQ** to orient you.  Joining a list can be like joining a secret society—you can make friends, enemies, a fool of yourself, a hash of your life, all in the course of an afternoon.  Subscribing to some lists (such as **cypherpunks)** may be like putting your lips to a firehose.

**LOL:**  Laughing Out Loud, in haqrspeak.

**lose, loser, loserhood, lossage**:  These are very general terms going back into the mists of programmerly history.  "Lose, lose" is a powerful **taunt**.

**lurk, lurker**:  Lurk and listen and keep your mouth shut to get your bearings in any **list** or **USENET** group.  Then you can learn what's going on without having to put yourself on the line… literally.  It's the equivalent of hanging around eavesdropping on a fascinating conversation at a party.  If you *never* contribute to the conversation after months and years, you're a lurker, which is like being a Peeping Tom.

**meat**: The physical body. Or, to meet someone in the flesh, **f2f**.

**meme**: A cultural quark. A little unit that assembles with others to build big ideas.

**modem**: Really means modulator/demodulator, and is the device that crams what you type on your keyboard into your telephone wire. Cherish your modem. It is the magic gate into **cyberspace**, a place much more satisfying than what they call the real world.

**mo'-dum**: What you get if you're always online and don't get mo' bettah.

**molybdenum**: A hard grey metallic element, atomic number 42, nickname Mo.

**MUD, MOO, MUSE**: A MUD is a real-time hangout place in cyberspace. MUDs (multi-user dungeons) are generally set up as Dungeons and Dragons games on steroids, where hundreds of simultaneous players explore exciting virtual territory, meet fascinating monsters, and kill them and confiscate their goods. MOOs focus on social interactions, and users can extend and reprogram the internal world in an object-oriented (OO) language. But a MUSE… well, never mind.

**narq**: A **defect**ive hacker. One who has passed over to the…

**narqside**: After **darqside**, what? Maybe *they* will discover your meat identity. When *they* come for your machines and take them all away, and take along your books and papers and plants and towels, and threaten to take away your life, you can let them take away your integrity too. Rat out your friends, why not? You've got some new friends now. They're nice, and they'll be your friends forever.

**nerd**: A programmer or other tech-knowledgeable person. Nerd is a glory term, not a curse. Nerdz are often **haqrz** and vice versa.

**Netcrawler, Netcrawling**: Tourism in cyberspace. Site-seeing. **Hyp-hop**ping from **Website** to Website and checking it all out.

**Netiquette**: Online etiquette. How you make no enemies accidentally, and anger only those you want to enrage. How not to make a fool of yourself or a hash of your life unless you really want to... Check **Netiquette**, Chapter Ten.

**newbie**: Someone who just figured out that this is the place to be, but doesn't know what to do here, yet. Newbies tend to use "Newbie" as a term of abuse against others. This is bullshirt. See **Advice to Newbies**, Chapter Eight.

**news groups**: These are ongoing conversations on **USENET** on a topic of mutual interest. News groups can be chitchat about cute things your pets have done or fiery revolutionary debates. Your choice.

**newtered**: A hacker made **celibate** against hir will.

**nightcrawling**: The seamy underside to **Netcrawling**. Prowling the Net looking for someone who seems to be of the appropriate sex who will exchange emessages of an intimate nature.

**NSA**: The (No Such Agency) aka National Security Agency. The NSA is responsible for protecting the government from people like you.

**online, The Online:** On The Wire, through the **modem**, in **cyberspace**.

**paper bag**: The cell to which **lamers** are confined—"you couldn't haxor yr way out of a paper bag."

**paranoia**: Up to a point makes one safer, beyond that point makes one stupider. See **mo'-dum.**

**PBX**: Private Branch Exchange. A local phone network, usually within a corporation. **Phreaker**s find an access number into a PBX, then dial an authorization code to get an outside line, in order to make illegal unlimited planetwide calls, toll-phree. Routing calls through multiple PBXs is done to dodge a trace.

**PGP**: Pretty Good Privacy, a **public key encryption** program that lets you encrypt your email, your cookbook, your hot **nightcrawling** sessions, your hard disk, and your life…

**phreaker**: A phone hacker. A musician who plays the phone keypad the way a **haqr** plays the keyboard.

**phun**: The real payoff for the true **haqr** or **phreaker**.

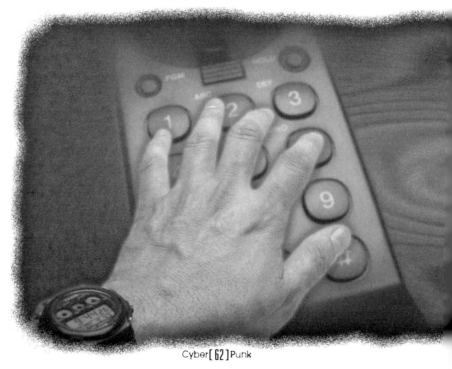

**pirating**: Hijacking the media. Pirating happens on any of the media... from audiotaping CDs to copying computer programs or distributing data without permission, from cracking the protection on computer games to broadcasting without an FCC license.

**pooh!**: A haqr endearment, used mostly in greetings: z1nky poooh!

**posse**: Some people you've met online who you talk to sometimes.

**procedural doodz**: See **cookbook guyz**.

**pseudonym**: Handle. Online name that may or may not be linked with your **meat** identity.

**public key encryption**: This is a nifty system for sending encrypted messages. A public-key encryption program like **PGP** makes you a pair of keys at the same time—your public key and your private key. You can distribute your public key everywhere, just like listing your number in a phone book. (People often add their public keys to their **dot.plan** files, or tack them on at the bottom of their email in their **dot.sig**.) Your private key you hold sacred. If people encrypt something with your public key they can be sure that only you can read it, because only you have your private key which can decrypt it.

**punk**: A rotten term for someone with a bad **attitude**. Or for someone who likes a certain style of music or clothes or books or food, or whatever the h*ck else. You know who you are.

**rad**:  Daring. Ingenious. Innovative. Illegal.

**ramen & Jolt**:  The haqr staffs of life.

**rancid**:  Useless. Disgusting. Not good. Whatever.

**remailers**: These are online sites that forward mail for you, incoming or outgoing. They're like online P.O. boxes. Using a remailer is a way of protecting your online identity. It lets you keep your **handle** from being linked with the **meat** you, or lets you function with complete **anonymity**.

**RFC**: The Internet exists only because our software believes in it. The RFCs—request for comments—are the technical specs for its operation. Anybody can write one, and they get approved by whoever shows up to the **IETF** to okay them. However, **bogus** decisions by the IETF can be ignored in practice, and then… it's like they never happened.

**ROFL**: Rolling On Floor Laughing.

**ROFLMAO**: Rolling On Floor Laughing My Buttocks Off.

**roll, roll over**: If you know what someone did, and who that someone is, **IRL**, and where they're doing other things, you can exchange this information for your own freedom in certain tight situations. But if you guard your own identity, and protect your friends' identities, and quit facin' other alpha-primates over virtual bananas, these situations will never arise, will they?

**root**: (from radix, Latin for root, as in "radical") That which underlies ordinary reality. Root, a mystical symbol like the Holy Grail, is the goal of haqrs everywhere and a source for **taunt**s: nya nya nya I got root at solar.sys.

**RSA**: Ron Rivest, Adi Shamir and Len Adelman are the guys who invented the most common scheme for **public key encryption.** RSA is used because Public Key Partners holds most patents on this flavor of encryption, and licenses only RSA. Also because RSA's so secure it gives the **NSA** cold sweats.

**RSI**: **Repetitive Stress Injury,** aka Carpal Tunnel Syndrome, is what can happen to you if you type too much. If you get this, the kewl thing to do is wear black leather wrist braces with chrome studs (BLWB-WCS). Hmm... although it might be better to get yr BLWBWCSs now, to fend off the RSI. Or best of all, just forget about typing, and wear your BLWBWCSs instead...

**sendmail**: A haqr's tool commonly mistaken for a UNIX system utility.

**shareware**: This is software on the honor system. You download it, you try it, you like it, you send the guyz who wrote it some $$.

**smart drugs**: These are supposed to augment the organ of highest importance in the Online—your brain. Maybe they work, maybe they don't. We don't want to influence you to buy strange chemicals at inflated prices so your estate can sue us. We don't want to spend the rest of our lives dodging your **AI** through cyberspace. We don't want any trouble.

**smileys**: Facial expressions shoved through the Wire. The first smiley was, of course, the Happy Face:

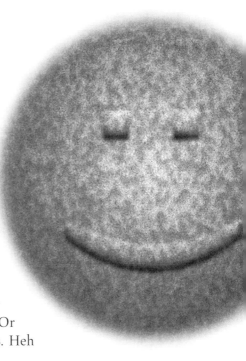

## :)

But then came the Leer ;)
the Unhappy Face : <
and too many others...
Write this in your cook-
book, bozo—NO SMILEYS.
Use a smiley, go to hail.
Smileys are dumb, smi-
leys are done, smileys
are RANCID. If you
can't make your read-
er realize that you're
not being serious, you
should forking hang it
UP. And that goes for
<grin> or <g> too. If you
want to be ironic or friendly
online, do it in WORDZ. Or
make up your OWN smileys. Heh
heh **heh**.

**smooch:**  Haqr endearment: >>smooch<<  See **pooh.**

**sniff, sniffer, sniffing**: Eavesdropping on the online. Mon-
itoring processes to see who's doing what. Used for and
against hacking. A sniffer might sniff traffic to sniff passwords, or to sniff a sniffer sniffing passwords. Got it?

**social engineering**:  Conning, juking, and sweet-talk-
ing favors or information (such as passwords or codes)
from company personnel by pretending to be a customer
or fellow employee in a jam. Honest **haqrz** will admit
that this is how they get most of their hacking info.

**spam**:   To overwhelm a communications medium.  A breach of **netiquette**. For example, emailing ads for your shyster law services to everyone on the Net. From the Monty Python skit where the menu was eggs, eggs and spam, eggs and spam and spam, and eggs and spam and spam, and spam, and spam, spam, spam, spam, spam, spam, spam, spam, spam, spam, spam, spam, spam, spam, spam, spam, spam, spam, spam, spam, spam, spam, spam, spam, spam, spam, spam, spam, spam, spam, spam, spam,
spam  spam  spam

s p a m

s p a m

s p a m

s p a m

s p a m

s p a m

s p a m

s p a m

s p a m

s p a m

s p a m

s p a m

spam spam

s p a m

spam spam

s p a m

s p a m

spam spam

spam spam spam

spam spam spam spam spam spam spam

spam spam spam spam spam spam spam spam spam

spam spam spam spam spam spam spam spam
spam, spam, spam, spam, spam, spam, spam
spam spam spam spam spam
spam spam spam spam spam
spam spam spam
spam spam
spam spam spam
spam spam spam
spam spam spam
spam
spam spam
spam spam
spam spam
spam spam
spam spam
spam
spam spam
spam, spam
spam spam
spamspam spam
spamspamspam
spamspam
spamspamspam
spam spam
spam spam
spam spam
spam
spamspamsp a
ammspamsp m

**spoof, spoofing**: Impersonation. Identity hacking. Pretending to be another sex, or age, or color, or weight, or ethicality, or someone else altogether. In the Net, eddressing hacks are called spoofs—all email from CliffStoll@cookie.monster.ah probably is a spoof. In **encryption**, spoofing is impersonating people in order to intercept their messages and break their codes.

**taunt**: Insult. Jeer at. Challenge. Another old-timey programmer term. Taunting is the online equivalent of fapping your enemy across the face with a glove. **Flame** wars start this way.

**trashing**: This is like **social engineering**—sneaky, yet informative. Trashing is going through someone's wastepaper basket, dumpster, or recycling bin to see what you can see.

**UNIX**: UNIX is no single unified thing, though it has but one name, with UNI in it yet. UNIX is legion, kludged from kludges, hacked from hacks. Imagine a construction site. UNIX is the scaffolding that programmers jerry-rigged in olden days to help them build a Great Unified System that would reach the heavens. But the scaffolding itself was just so… useful… to programmers. They could do everything they needed to do in there, and if they couldn't they'd bash together another ladder or lay some planks across a beam— okay, so it wasn't Great or Unified, but what the håck, it was home… And as years went by they forgot all about building the Great System, and squatted in the kipple, and UNIX remains, to this very day, a dark endless maze of catwalks and mantraps, an eternal hard-hat area that kills the foolish and shelters the brave.

**URL**: Universal Resource Locator. This is a WWW eddress, a nexus in the Big Web. URLs usually look something like http://www.something/something.html. Nowadays Netcrawlers exchange URLs instead of email addresses as a mark of status. At the next table you hear cyber-yups jabbering "http colon slash slash" and you know what's going on. Wanna hear what the O.J. Simpson Homepage URL is? http://////////////. That's sick.

**Usenet**: A distributed electronic BBS, only this one is distributed planet-wide. You can sign on and read postings from people all over the world on topics from the inane to the diabolical. You can add your own thoughts. (Advisable to think first.)

**valorize**: Rationalize something with so many footnotes that it might as well be valid. This is an academic term, used in academe by academics.

**VMB**: Voice Mail Box. The **phreaker's** playground. Daring phreakers like to use the VMBs of the *phone company itself* for a voice-mail drop, like a voice-based BBS. Phreakers can leave voice messages with news, callingcard or creditcard numbers, new codez, or other goodies to be shared around.

**warez**: Software, pirated or waiting to be pirated. Some BBSes are warez boredz, with collections of pirated software to be downloaded.

**warez kidz**: Those who download pirated software to add to their collections. Among **hacker**s information is status. Among the warez kidz, the actual *software* is status—but it's got to be completely current, and you **lose** if it's not pre-release or hard to find.

**Website**: The there that's there behind the **URL**. See **homepage**.

**win, winnage**: Another ancient haqr concept. As the easy opposite of **lose**, win is usually used ironically, as in *"There's* a big win," but don't be fooled. Winnage is almost as important as **information** itself.

**woo!**: An exclamation of haxor glee that sounds ironic but isn't. It's glee. Sometimes repeated or encased in **bang**s: !!w00w00!!

**WWW—World-Wide Web**:    The conceptual BigNet. Everything connected to everything, but WITH REAL PHOTOS and non-**ASCII** GRAFIX!  But wait!  WWW's too *easy*!  **Lamers** and **losers** can find their way around instantly, and do *everything* in the Web!  Hackerly skills are useless!  The **haqr ethic** is meaningless!  Web Browsing is just Site-seeing!!!  It's like going through the whole planet in a TOUR BUS!!!  AAAAAaaaaaaa.

# Building Your Cyber Word Power, cont'd

## Part 2: *A Cyberpunk Phrasebook, With Hip Conversational Ploys for Winning Without a Clue*

Did you seriously believe we could help you with this? What a pathetic **loser**!
Forget about just spouting the cybercrap, because

1. If you're up against somebody who knows hir stuff, you're doomed.
2. And if you're talking to somebody who doesn't know ruffled shirt, why keep spouting?

In either case, you'd best can the cyberspeak. You want to learn from people who know things, and impress people who don't, right? Okay—so make both categories laugh, or show them your leathers. Buy them a drink. Don't bother me about this again, you hear?

# Chapter 5
# Cheatcards for Books
# You Should Have Read
*But Didn't*

**Neuromancer**
by William Gibson
A high-tech and very poignant, poetic romance—boy loses machine, boy meets girl with built-in mirrorshades and retractable razor fingernails, boy loses girl, boy loses everything, boy gets machine.

*Neuromancer* is the book that made the genre, sort of. YOU MUST READ THIS BOOK.
Four shuriken.

THE BOOK OF THE YEAR!
WINNER OF THE HUGO, NEBULA AND PHILIP K. DICK AWARDS!

NEUROMANCER
**WILLIAM GIBSON**

"KALEIDOSCOPIC, PICARESQUE, FLASHY AND DECADENT...AN AMAZING VIRTUOSO PERFORMANCE...STATE-OF-THE-ART!"
—*WASHINGTON POST*

## Schismatrix

by Bruce Sterling

A thriller about the future war between those who wanna tinker with widgets vs. those who wanna tinker with their bodies. This is an insanely funny book masquerading as SERIOUS INTELLIGENT FICTION, and I'm sorry I mentioned it for a cheatcard, just read it.

Four shuriken.

## Snow Crash

by Neal Stephenson

Neal Stephenson is a latecomer to the Cyberpunk Pantheon, but he's right up there. The first chapter of this book has been beamed into space in 70 languages. Hail, you gotta read this one, too. It's okay, you'll like it.

Four shuriken.

## True Names

by Vernor Vinge

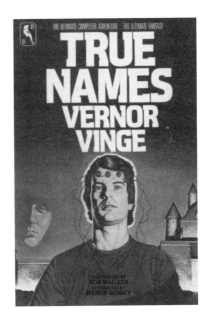

This is a classic that Vernor Vinge wrote a long time ago, but is completely uptodate and intelligent and moreover kicks butt. The best editions of this book have an afterword by Marvin Minsky that explains how plausible this book is from the Artificially Intelligent standpoint. It doesn't get much better than this. Okay, you have to read this one, too.

Four shuriken.

*Okay, okay, I take it back about the cheat-cards—read ALL these books, immediately. Read* Neuromancer *too, even though I've given away the plot.*

## Software and Wetware
by Rudy Rucker

Rudy Rucker is the only one of the original cyberpunks who actually knows his shirt. Programming, hacking, cellular automata, artificial life… you name it, Rudy can DO it. He's Hegel's grand-nephew, and a real mathematician, and can be heard at cyberpunk parties moaning over the comparative size of his and William Gibson's advances, "He may write better than I do, but he doesn't write *a thousand times better*." Read the *Warez* books and decide for yourself. Three shuriken.

## Eclipse Trilogy
by John Shirley

Shirley is the ultimate guy-type guy in a guy-type-guy's genre. His *Eclipse* books feature epic struggles of good and evil, freedom and fascism, rock and roll. Shirley also wrote the first script for *The Crow* before they added all the splatter, so you can't bust him for this one. He's writing for movies and TV because cyberpunk writers don't get paid shirt for their novels. 'Cept for Gibson.

Three shuriken.

### Shockwave Rider

by John Brunner

Proto-cyberpunk tale written (in 1973!!) about a young upscale hacker brat who **spoof**s himself new identities like you change your socks. This book supposedly inspired the infamous Internet Worm that tied up 6,600 computers and cost Internet users an estimated 90 million dollars. My goodness, what damage a mere book can do! PUT THIS DOWN AND GO WASH YOUR HANDS! Four shuriken and four beanies!!

and

# Chapter 6
# Cheatcards For Movies/TV
# You Didn't See
*But Should Know About*

## Bladerunner

Come *on*. Until you've seen *Bladerunner*, we're not even going to talk to you. *Bladerunner* is a crash course in cyberpunk. It's even more brilliant than the novel, which is actually a short story. Well, there's the novel *Do Androids Dream of Electric Sheep* by Philip K. Dick, which *Bladerunner*'s not really based on, but its title's from a William S.

Burroughs short story that pre-saged the narco-realpolitik of our times. Say that until you get it right. There's a Website that deals with this flick—go to http://kzsu. stanford.edu/uwi/br/off-world.html Four shuriken and four propeller beanies!!

## Terminators 1-7

Or so. Monster truck-pull movies with trillion-dollar budgets and ARNIE as one of the trucks. Post-apocalyptic L.A. Steroid mutant superstar. Skip directly to *T2*. Killer special effects. Tough hero chick and her ATM-hacking pre-pubescent son. Super-morphing cyborg bad guy turns to a puddle on the floor and back again in this ultraviolent tribute to Mandelbrot sets. Only in America. Only in these times. One to four shuriken, we can't remember.

## Alien 1 and 3, Aliens

Science-fiction-horror-war movies. Sigourney Weaver as a Marine grunt in skivvies, with guns. Ultrahip Giger designer paraphernalia. Great stuff.

Four shuriken.

## Fire in the Streets

Amy Madigan is the dysgruntled grunt, fully battle-dressed, lots o' guns here too. Willem Dafoe in latex overalls, yow.

Two shuriken and a yow.

## Johnny Mnemonic

William Gibson's screenplay adaptation of his short story of that title, from his short story collection, *Burning Chrome*. This is a motion picture with a serious moral: if you somehow offend the gods of cyberspace (see **Sects** in the special censored section) They'll have Hollywood make a movie from your dreams

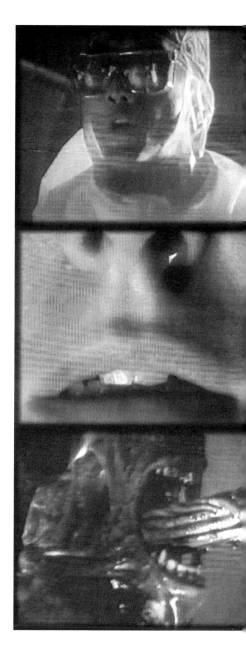

and cast Keanu Reeves as the hero. Go out and buy *Burning Chrome*, crawl into bed and read *all* his short stories. Two shuriken, one beanie.

## Max Headroom

If there IS a god, He, She or It has a video of the original Max Headroom—yes, the British version—on hir VCR. "It's the future—humans as data."... brought to you by Pepsi. MH is haqr smarts in action. The stuff going on the background is more interesting than the main plot of most movies. Aaaieeee.

Four shuriken and four beanies.

## Sneakers

Aptly-named flick about hacking the banking system. It sneaked the ultimate truth about our social structure into a popular mainstream movie—"Money doesn't exist anymore. It's an illusion. It's just bits and bytes." Dan Ackroyd has a supporting role as a paranoid conspiracy freek, which he actually is. Just thought you should know that. Fun.

Only two shuriken but four beanies.

## WarGames

Good kid hacker with cute and earnest girlfriend almost launches nuclear war from his home computer in the 'burbs. Liberal Hollywood film, lite ethical hand-wringing, hap-

py ending.  No, we actually *like* this movie.  Honest.
Two shuriken.

**Escape From New York, Total Recall, Scanners,** and Lots
of Others We Can't Remember
Unmemorable, but cyber.
Two shuriken… probably.

**Tron**
First use of great computer graphics in an idiotic movie.
Guy gets stuck inside a life-or-death nasty videogame.
John Lilly, the cosmic dolphin dude, said this movie was
"about the dilemmas I face in my philosophy."  Remember, kids, on ketamine and cocaine you can find the meaning
of life in an episode of *Power Rangers*.  NOT recommended.  The movie either.
One shuriken… maybe.

 ?

**Tetsuo: The Iron Man**
An average shaving Japanese guy discovers that one of
his beard hairs is now a wire—or maybe he's got a steel
zit—and his eyes bug in horror, and the soundtrack tens-
es up… and over the course of an hour he slowly breaks
out all over his body with wires and cables and other scrap,
as the soundtrack goes all *Eraserhead*.  The plot sickens,
sexy Japanese people chop off their own and others' body
parts and post-body non-parts, and menace each other

with Allen wrenches and volt-meters. It devolves into a cyborgy… If they were 100% flesh, it could be obscene. As is, it's only the dream that Mark Pauline will never see a therapist about. Mark Pauline? Ask any black-clad young adult in your local **boho** district. Only one thumb up—I gave it one *finger*—but call it two shuriken.

### Videodrome

Deborah Harry has a video-tape inserted into her stomach. That's all you need to carry you through a **Con** conver-sation. That and the name of the *auteur*… Cronenberg. David Cronenberg. Watch-ing his entire *oeuvre* of psychobiological-mutation horror flicks in one night on Brainwash can turn you into an INHUMAN MUTANT FREAK for *life*. Hee hee hee hee. Well, *pith my viscera*. Three shuriken.

## Reboot

This is a TV cartoon that THEY are trying to keep from you by showing it at 8:30 AM—on *Saturday morning*. Imagine computer animations that parody Lucasfilm and Spielberg and Giger—chrome everywhere, vehicles going much too fast in tight spaces, along with the best facial renderings ever. Imagine er- an intelligent *Speed Racer??* A spoof of nerd culture to the last low-order bit. **Lamers** in *Reboot* get called *dipswitch!* Watch the backgrounds closely.

Three propeller beanies.

# Chapter 7
# Online Things You
# Should Know About
## *Even if You Never*
## *Go Online*

Oh, forget about this. Just get your az online, somehow, anyhow, right now. Knowing about this is NOT ENOUGH. You must DO it! The next section will get you up to speed. You GOTTA GET ONLINE. Turn the page!!!!

# SECTION 3

## [ CYBERPUNK... DOING IT! ]

# Chapter 8
# Art of the Hack for Beginners
*A Child's First Book of Piracy, Intrusion, and Espionage*

## Advice to Newbies

First, don't worry about knowing nothing. Everybody starts out as a newbie. The point is not to stay one.

Hang out on **list**s and news groups where people know things. Download the **FAQ**s you find there. Save the FAQs. Read them. They will give you enough background to understand the topics you're interested in. Follow the conversations online, but resist your urge to blab—just stop, lurk and listen. Then, if you've researched, pondered, and you still don't understand something, ASK A QUESTION. Chances are that others need enlightenment on this point too, but are afraid to ask. Do not fear being jeered at if you ask a good question. The ones most likely to jeer at you and call you newbie are other newbies mortified by their condition. These newbies are **losers**. They will learn nothing and they will STAY newbies.

So, you ask good questions, you thank people who give you answers, and you save the answers with the FAQs... and you start your own online notebook. Don't worry about being a **cookbook** d00d. What kind of cramp is that? You afraid someone will think you're a newbie? You ARE a newbie. Get over it. What do you think, did Phiber Optik, haqr god, start out as a newbie, or did he spring full-grown from a circuit diagram?
NEWBIE NEWBIE NEWBIE NEWBIE.
You over it yet?

### Haqr Mind
What do you think, are we about to say something like, "Grasshopper, Haqr mind... is very like... Zen mind"?????
Forget it. Haqr mind is NOTHING like Zen mind. Haqr mind is what Buddhists snottily call MONKEY MIND. Imagine your mind has four hands and a prehensile tail, and can climb over or through anything. Even more fun, imagine your mind has eight tentacles, or twenty... twenty glutinous, translucent tentacles, with suckers on them, exuding a slime that dissolves anything...

### Haqr Smarts
Use everything you've got. Then use everything you can get, online and off. If you need some information, be cunning and cool. Work up your **social engineering** skills. Cherish your data when you get it. Archive it. Encrypt it. Wring implications out of it... see what else might work and try it out. Think! Explore! Think some more! When a reporter asked Sir Isaac Newton (this is

true, shut up a minute) how he came up with his Theory of Gravitation, Newton said, "By thinking about it unceasingly." Yo!

## Social Engineering for Fun and Profit

Most haqrs will admit that almost all of their insider information comes from social engineering. This is the way they score passwords to accounts, get phone numbers that do kewl things, and find out where the bodies are buried. They call up after office hours and pretend to be consultants who have forgotten the password... or linemen who need to check on this or that. The ethics of this SUX. Conning people is NOT nice. It isn't. Flimflamming people into betraying their company's proprietary information is dastardly. Moreover, these people you're juking ARE nice, probably very nice, just like your own family. The sales rep you weasel the password out of might be just like your brother. Your bigger brother. The one who tormented you all through your childhood...

CRETS
by The Knightmare

introduction by Gareth Branwyn

OF A

SUPER

ACKER

# Chapter 9
# The Hardware/Software
# You Actually Need
*Or How to Fake It*

## Get That Motherboard Outa Here

Now we get to the hard stuff. We must now talk frankly about computers. If you're gonna do anything really cyber with your life—you must get a computer. It's not easy to think about, but you gotta do it. You can sort of ease up to computers by finding yourself a Macintosh. The Macintosh is not intrinsically lame. No. Although it is a very good machine for newbies, because when you plug it all together it works. Instantly. And it takes almost no ramp-up time for you to learn it, either. What's the fun in that? you might ask. Well, it means you start out hacking stuff more interesting than how to subjugate MS-DOS, and what to do when cables have one wrong end—can you believe this has SEVENTEEN PRONGS?

A Macintosh allows you to make some of your breadth requirements in life. Time out from sockets! You can hack your environment in artistic ways. On a Mac you can procrastinate endlessly while building your artistical skills—drawing gnarly icons, hanging your own skull-spangled Wallpaper, or recording cool things for your computer to say instead of "Beep." If you long to be someday among the ascended masters of UNIX, get Mach-10—a cheap UNIX for Macs—and work your way up. But while you're on the Mac side, there are benefits. Get FTPd, which is Mac shareware, and there you are—you're part of the Net. FTPd makes you almost unhackable, because intruders coming in meet an alien Macintosh interface, which boggles their minds beyond belief. MacHTTP, also **shareware**, makes you a **Website.**

Macs can be expensive, even second-hand, because until now nobody could buy a new cheap Macintosh knockoff… but this will happen. In the meantime, check with Macintosh User Groups for cast-offs.

After all this buildup about Macs, if your poverty or bad luck forces you to adopt a thrashed-out IBM clone with Megadeth stickers all over it… well, that's life. Get LINUX instantly, and you got your UNIX, sort of.

*Cybertip: If you hassle hardware, keep in mind that Phiber Optik, widely believed to be god of the hack, performed software miracles on a tiny obsolete Commodore. Yes.*

## Forget That, Macs *Are* Lame
### *(A Minority Opinion, Thanks to Douglas Barnes)*

Macs are easy (which is why lameaxes like Jude and R.U. like them so much), but they insulate you from the gory component-level HARDWARE hackery, and it's all that card swapping, IRQ fiddling, dip-switch setting, chip pulling, and tooth gnashing that make the Intel-based PC world *very* cyberpunk. Using a Mac makes it a hurl of a lot harder to achieve **deep geek**hood, and you're far less likely to build up really neat piles of old interface cards, motherboards, and obsolete hard drives. (Although the old Macs had their own weird tools JUST TO OPEN THEM UP which you could leave lying around to look like you were diversifying into open-heart surgery.)

Also, you never hear of people building a Mac from components variously purchased from three catalogs, borrowed from friends and retrieved from the dumpster behind Joe's PC Palace and Bait Shop. YOU CAN DO THIS WITH IBM PCs, and then scatter any extra parts around your home or apartment to give it that cyberpunk je ne sais quoi...

Novelist Umberto Eco compared the Mac operating system to the Catholic church. Believers (users) must approach God (the hardware) through a layer of churchy indirection and simplification (icons, symbols, point-and-click), while DOS is very Protestant—you're responsible for achieving salvation ON YOUR OWN, dimmit, and you confess your sins directly to GOD, AND NO KISSY-FACE ICONS IN BETWEEN.

*Cybertip:  Bear in mind, of course, that arguing about hardware is what the true cyberpunk does instead of following professional sports.*

## Which Modem and Why

Get the fastest modem you can afford. Fast. Cheap. Shop around, buy by mail if you have to.  Being online at too low a speed is very frustrating, like eating peas with chopsticks.  Modems list their speeds in baud rates, which is not really bits per second but might as well be.  Go for 14.4K or higher or else.  Speed is going up all the time. Keep up with it.

## Encryption Programs

PGP (Pretty Good Privacy) is the grand-daddy hero of them all.  Phil Zimmerman is the maniac reponsible, and several federal agencies are hankering to put him away. PGP, it turns out, is TOO Good Privacy, and real encryption is classed along with munitions—if it's any good, it's illegal to export it.  Since PGP was posted to the USENET, which is as international as anything can get, the feds are very cross with Phil Zimmerman.  FTP the latest version of PGP from the sites listed on http://www.four11.com/. This is the page for The World-Wide Web Virtual Library: Cryptography, PGP, and Your Privacy, so you can look around for other stuff while you're there.

**Email programs that incorporate PGP** are now being developed. These will allow you to encrypt your email automagically, which is much better than sending your email out naked into the world. Check the privacy sites for them as well.

## Terminally Hip Extras

### Laptops
These are truly useful. If you just pack your laptop down to the corner or make an appointment to sit under a tree, it gets you away from your squalid little room, ne? Three-and-a-half shuriken, four shuriken if you get it second-hand, cheap.

### Heads-Up Display
This is like a Walkman for your eyes. It looks like an LED version of the little rearview mirrors that bicyclists wear on their heads, but it displays your monitor screen *right into your eye*. Insanely dangerous in traffic, it nonetheless looks SO CYBER. This is funny tech. It looks intimidating. It can kill you. Sounds to me like three shuriken.

### Personal Communicators

This is an example of **futurespoofing**. It's a really good idea, and it doesn't quite work, and it's very, very expensive. How could you resist? Two shuriken until further notice.

### Scrambler Cell Phone

Your neighborhood may contain perverts who listen in to cellular phone calls. Some of them may wear uniforms. Whoever they are, drive them mad with a scrambler. Scrambler cell phones are still monstrously expensive, because nobody buys them, since nobody in this country believes in privacy yet. If you can't afford a *scrambler* cell phone, don't touch a cell phone, ever.

Either

### Cellular Email/Fax

Same thing. Read it or weep.

Either

### Beeper/Pager

This is sorta old-tech—it's passé, yes, but it's useful and cheap. Don't disdain useful and cheap. Morons are taken in by expensive and glittery and NEW NEW NEW. For that sort of thing, settle for the next category and save big $$.

Old tech, good stuff.

### Realistic Balsa Mockups
### of the Above, and Other Hip Stuph

Wearing these nonchalantly will impress people who love widgets for their own sake. If you *want* to impress these people. It's your life.

# Chapter 10
# Your Online Persona
*How to Win Friends,*
*Score Information,*
*and Intrigue the*
*Apposite Sex*

## Starting Out Right

### Writing a Kewl dot.plan

Write one! Right now! It posses me off when I can't **finger** somebody's dot.plan so I'll know who the fork I'm talking to, even if the information is totally **bogus.** Okay? Okay, what should you say in it? Cool quotes expressing your entire philosophical underminings are fine, but essays are wearying. Brevity is good. Succinct, spare, minimal, terse. Curt.

### Designing a Non-lame dot.sig

Keep in mind that everybody has to read this dim thing at the bottom of every single posting of yours, and again at the end of every single **emsg** they get from you. A dot.sig might be changed now and then, like socks. An elaborate and beautiful **ascii** dot.sig might make some people envious… or they may just envy you all the leisure you've got if you can make ASCII grafix SO PERFECT.

Here's an example of a tasteful and info-rich dot.sig:

```
"There's no second chance when FORTRAN is used for EVIL!"
```

## Location, Location, Location: What Your Eddress Says About YOU

Okay, we're talking snob. How do you deal with the sort of person who will judge you by what you can afford to rent, either **IRL** or online? For snob appeal, consider the dot.edu. Haqrs often have dot.edu eddresses, by finding a comfortable space somewhere in the virtual basement of a large university and just moving in. A squatted edu eddress is intrinsically tony… but think of the possibilities… princeton.edu?!

If you have to *buy* your way onto an online service, consider a great grey server like netcom. ANYONE might live there… it's neutral turf, no blame. Idiotproof servers like US OnLine are like traveling by bus… there are too many people in line ahead of you, and most of them you'd rather not end up sleeping next to. But if you want to impress a connoisseur of eddresses, a real esnob, choose a service run by former haqrs, especially ones who got indicted.

Above and beyond, the truly snob-proof way to be online is TO BE the online—to have your machine act as an Internet node. This is expensive so far, but it's clearly the way of the future. Being your own node is like having your own telephone, instead of sharing a party line with hippie farmers, or using the pay phone in the deli downstairs.

## Beyond Attitude... *What??*
## Netiquette

We don't have the pages here to be the real Ms. Manners of Cyberspace. We can only cue you a little, as you totter your first steps through the online scene. With practice, you will find yourself turning away wrath or sarcasm gently, with good taste and nicely-veiled threats. Here's a real-life example:

```
From: simcere@nanodix.org
Subject: About Cyberpunk?
Dear Ms.Stjude
    I was looking at some text written by
you at Gopher.well.sf.ca.us/cyberpunk, and I
must say I found it very interesting but con-
fusing.  My question is then, what is this
thing cyberpunk?  How can I get into it?
Because It sounded like something I would
have to get into.


Yours sincerly
Mr Bungle


********************************************T
here is nothing so useless as doing effi-
ciently that which should not be done at all.
—Peter F. Drucker
*******************************************
```

```
To: simcere@nanodix.org
Subject: Re:  About Cyberpunk?

Dear Mr. Bungle,

Could it be that you are NOT writing
sincerly, at all?  That you are being
sarcastic?  I have been sarcastic myself,
oh yes.  And I know how to do many cyber
things.  It would be sad if you were
attacking me with sarcasm.

Imagine waking up in the small hours—say 9
AM—with a thick Latvian banker on the phone
demanding to know where is limo, is late? or
a sweet voice sobbing that you must page
Russell Knight, age 8, to report to the Avis
desk.  Life is chock with event when you
have a white courtesy telephone.

But no: you really want to know the things
that I am writing in THE REAL CYBERPUNK
FAKEBOOK!  And, yes, you can!  There's a
cornucopia of data, for those who NEED TO
KNOW, and it's all
yours, VERY sincerly,

>jude<
```

## Art of the Flame: When and Why, and If So, How

If some marron keeps ON getting in your face you'll be
tempted to bash hirm with adjectives, nouns, and adverbs
we can't use here. Don't. Be cool. Show up hir faulty
logic and stark presumption in a few spare lines. Be cool-
ly superior in a minimal way. Dry, wry, and sly. It drives
them nuts.

*Cybertip: Make no enemies accidentally. Choose your enemies as carefully as you choose your friends. A truly contemptible enemy is as useful as a cool friend. A well-known azole who hates you loudly and often will keep your name before the public in a positive way.*

## Online Poise: Cool in a MUD, Uncowed in a MOO

Think before you type. Don't be an azole. Keep your calm. CALM DOWN.

# Chapter 11
# How To Avoid
# Bankruptcy

This was only a dumb joke to put in the Table of Contents.
Just turn the page to…

# Chapter 12
# Where to Hang
*Finding the Cool Places*
*in Cyberspace*

## Will the Web Kill Hacking?

The Web is loaded with amenities. It's like a four-star tour. And that's why the Web may kill haqrhood.

There's the membership problem. **Haqr** society is like the Shakers—the community can't grow by the usual primate strategy—biological reproduction is right out—so its continuation depends on the faithful going out and bringing in new recruits from the general population. Yes, we're saying it out loud: Haqrs recruit. Haqrs are intrinsically subversive to the young. Haqrs are conscious role models for haqr glory. If that weren't enough, haqrs actively seek to convert the imaginative and the credulous to their lifestyle. Haqrs could be barred from hosting scout troops of any gender.

Okay, but look where the new recruits are coming from, nowadays. This younger generation is accustomed to the hot-towel amenities of Netscape. Haqr is toughness. Gutz. It's like boot camp, the ultimate challenge for a few good persons. Haqrhood depends on people wanting and NEEDING to root around in UNIX sub-basements— down there with the dripping pipes and rats and spiders, and no amenities at all.

And, even as we speak, oldstyle haqr d00dz are pouring out from those cellars and spending good haq time just coasting around on Netscape. Arrrhhhh.

*Time out for a cyber-rant: The Web! What is the Web but a bunch of static dioramas like in the Natural History Museum, all the exhibits all very handy and online, but still exhibits—like a Funhouse where things light up or jump out at you but are still flat and lifeless and always THE SAME… AAAAAAA, it's like being trapped in Disneyland!!!!!*

Okay, I'm ready to go on now. Here are some kewl sites.

**Computer underground Digest** has a great URL, which is the trail head for all kinds of interesting excursions into the Web. Fire up yr Netscape and go to
http://sun.soci.niu.edu/~cudigest/
You'll find links to crypto sites, strange homepages, all kindsa neat stuph.

**Phrack Magazine**, a long-time haq/phreak online zine, has a site with back issues and an under-construction link for underground resources.
http://freeside.com/phrack.html (Phrack WWW Home Page)

**Crypt Newsletter** is an E-zine addressing social and political issues of computer culture. George Smith, Editor.
http://sun.soci.niu.edu/~crypt/

For a quick tour through the hypest in weird—and to find trail heads to endless paths of possibility across the Web, try Mitchell Porter's **Hyper-Weirdness by E-Mail v2.2** at
http://phenom.physics.wisc.edu/~shalizi/hyper-weird/

For some good graphical exploration, stop by the **Mind-Vox World Wide Web Server**
http://www.phantom.com/

Go immediately to:
http://abominable.winternet.com:80/~drow/
This will enmesh you in **Demon Web**, the work of the demonic drow—actual haqr, inventor of the eleet and morse code philterz for **irc**, and hell's angel of the information highway. Check every single thing that drow recommends, but when you come to the end and see
PRESS THIS BUTTON!

*Don't.*

**CastleVoid!**
<URL:http://www.phantom.com/~voidmstr>
Voidmstr says the Web right now is like the underground/progressive radio of the very early 1970s—a brand-new medium waiting to be explored, pirated, bent and twisted. Voidmstr did the grafix for the MINDVOX sites, and is fairly twisty himself:
Voidmstr's Law (tm) states:
Bandwidth expands to fit the waste available

The Voidmstr sez—
"If people weren't filling up the World Wide Web with
self-indulgent effluvia like this, we would all still be
calling local dial-ups at 300 baud, typing in ALL
CAPS +l=l!Nl<1l\lG W3 \\/3l~3 1<3\\/L."


## IRCs

Try the #hack channels. When you're online, in the loving arms of UNIX, type irc.
This will put you into the Internet Relay Chat. Then
you type
/join #hack

The irc program will come back at you snottily:
*** Topic for #hack: Wannabees need not apply

Or worse yet:
#hack Sorry, cannot join channel. (Invite only channel).

Okay for that channel. Fork 'em if they can't take a
newbie. Instead you can try
/join #hack2
or any other number. This should get you into something strange. You'll see things like, "it probably uses all
the same holes that the 8lgm stuff does." And other
eye-watering flimmery that makes you wonder why
you're here. That's okay. Just try another channel. To
find out which channels are available, do
/list
This will print out a list of channels available worldwide.
Some of them have explanatory notes next to them.
These notes are often in strange and seductive lan-

guages. Don't mess with them unless you're prepared to speak this language to whoever's there. Some channels have perverts waiting in them like spiders for a fly. Don't mess with these unless you're prepared to cope with what they're inviting you to, and can type well under stressful conditions.

On the hack channels, lurk around. Lurk, but don't touch. Learn how things are done, don't draw any fire, choose yr friends and enemies tentatively... because as time goes by they may switch places with each other.

## BBSes

Try your local BBSes, for starts. Since they're in your area, maybe eventually you might **meat** some of the people on them. **F2f** is always weird. You talk with your minds online, so bodies are a shocking afterthought.

## MUDs & MOOs & MUSEs

These are changing all the time. It's like clubs—they're born and they die. Turnover is the rule. Fall into the Web. Follow your nose.

## Special Interest Groups (With a Special Word About alt.sex.bestiality)

The alt.dot groups on USENET are famous. Some of them get corralled into Mitchell Porter's **Hyper-Weirdness by Email**, and some of them roam free. Alt.sex is like the Adult Bookstore across the tracks. Everybody complains about it, but everyone wants a peek, just a peep...

Now, alt.sex.bestiality is actually a charming place to peek into. It's full of people who are romantically interested in animals. Very sincere people. They are NOT interested in crass one-night stands. They want long-term committed relationships based on mutual respect and understanding. With fully-consenting animals only. So sweet.

# SECTION IV: CYBERPUNK...

## [ CYBERPUNK... THE SCENE ]

# Chapter 13
# Face Time
*Pleased to Meat You?*

## Hacking Your Face2face IRL Persona

Second-hand stores are good for everything you need. Don't be too proud to buy stuph second-hand. Used things always look cooler than brand-plastic new. Second things are unique. And cheap. Some of them may fit.

## The Mandatory Black Leather Jacket

A novice cyberpunk may consider zippered leather a sine qua nono. Actually, your Black Leather Jacket (BLJ) is symbolic. It could just as well be made from some shiny supersynthetic. Or think denim, weezil pelts, or rubber. Innovative fabrics and designs for your BLJ show you fear nothing. **Lamer**s may later make a fad out of your polystyrene or your aluminum chainlink,

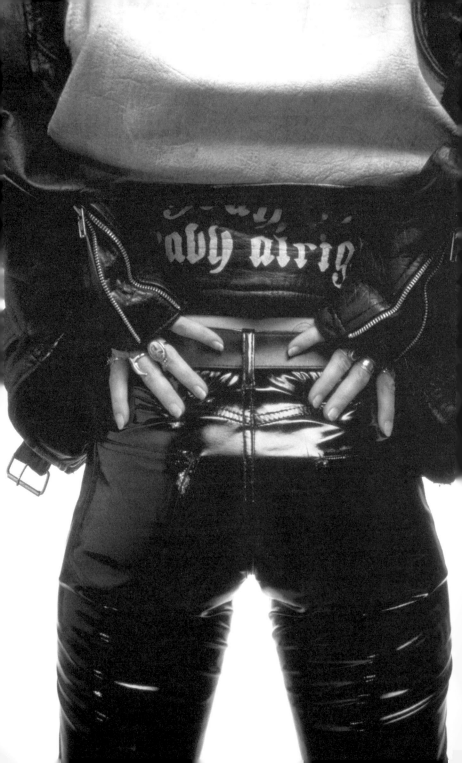

but you had the conans to wear it first. The real requirements for a BLJ are two:

1. It has many secure pockets, and

2. Even if it's a difficult wear, it seems very natural on you—as if you've bathed in it for years.

### Leather Trousers?

Talk about a difficult wear! Leather Trousers are unmatched
for comfort this side of the iron maiden, and in fact, LTs
do have spikes inside. Anyone wearing them has GOT
to be cool, because LTs DEFINE Harsh. Actually, you
needn't bother. See previous.

### Boots

Boots are, in fact, mandatory, but you have options here,
too. Your first bets are either skintight and shiny, or big
and brutal. Think intimidation, comfort, and protection.
Be strategic about your Boots. Have a couple of pairs. Plan
out your needs. You can predict you'll need steel toes for
musical events and technical discussions.

## Hair

Dreads are good right now, especially if you're caucasian, as are braided hair extensions that go to great lengths, like your elbows. Shaving parts of your skull is always good. Dyeing what's left of your hair in very electric, unhairlike colors is good. Blue is not yet cliché, especially that clear lovely blue. Blue shows all skin-colors to good advantage. Mmm… blue hair.

## Wearable Electronics: What's Chic, What's Rancid?

and also

## Buttons/Badges/Insignia, With a Special Warning About StarFleet Gear

Forget about *all* this stuff. Really. Even if you're in Los Angeles and have to wade hipdeep through the ambient Boole-ship, there's no point to buying widgets to wear, or spiking trendy cruft through your leathers. Phorque all that. Go sit somewhere congenial and read yr UNIX manual.

### Street Cred and Martial Arts

Street cred is difficult for nerds. On the street, big and strong wins. If you're concerned about instilling respect—even fear—into other primates, you know that big and strong is only relative. Which doesn't help you at all, even with martial arts.

Listen—if you square off with somebody who's willing to kiyai with you, they probably have a couple of *dans* UP on you, and all the arts you can martial will not keep them from stomping your ash. Learning martial arts *and* packing a large calibre weapon may help, but no. Stay *off* that street. If you have to go buy more Jolt, walk softly and carry a big intellect. Remember that cats and other predators chase anything that flees them, and flee anything that chases them. Do not scuttle like a prey, *stalk like a predator.* If you can't walk, talk or attitude your way out of a bad situation, SCREAM.

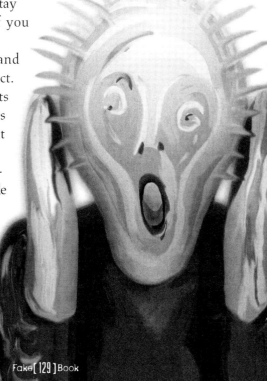

# Chapter 14
# Terminally Hip Widgets
## *and High-Tech ToyZ*

### Fun With Your Cellular Phone

Yes, you can listen in to your neighbors' conversations on your cellular phone. If your neighbors are like ours, this won't be fun. You could have a more interesting time drawing gnarly skulls for your Wallpaper program or trying to get root at NASA. Just kidding.

### One Hundred Uses for a Laser Pointer!

Actually, we can't think of even one use for a laser pointer. Who the håck said you hafta have a laser pointer, anyway? Question Authority? Says WHO????

## Laminator 2: Identity Hacking

Hacking your own identity is fun. Having a badge that claims you're a security expert, for example, and which appears to give you access to all areas without an armed escort. A small laminating machine is not all that cheap, but you'll offset some of the cost by making up security badges for your friends. Here is a phun design:

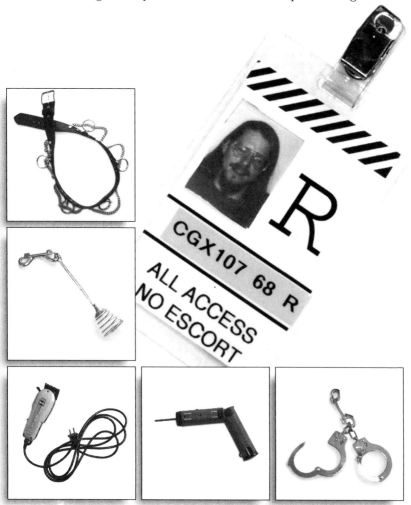

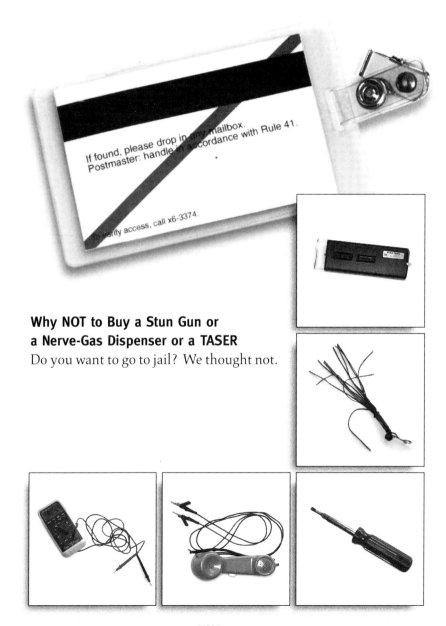

If found, please drop in any mailbox.
Postmaster: handle in accordance with Rule 41.

To verify access, call x6-3374.

## Why NOT to Buy a Stun Gun or a Nerve-Gas Dispenser or a TASER

Do you want to go to jail? We thought not.

# Chapter 15
# Games!
*Video Games,*
*Computer Games &*
*Offline Games*

## Part 1: Video Games & Computer Games

These games divide easily into categories. Either they train your monkey reflexes so you can grow up to be a fighter pilot, or they prey upon your monkey curiosity and competitiveness. Which kind of primate are you?

### Fast-Twitch Muscle Games: Mortal Combat, Doom, etc

This is a way to lose a lot of time out of your life, but these things are PHUN. Along about the third week, you might ask yourself, what am I doing here? Am I trying to get really *really* good at shooting reptile Marines with a mouse, or am I figuring out how this works? The haqrly mind takes things apart to analyze them. A phairly phamous haqr friend sets these games at the lowest level of difficulty and then just cruises around checking out the territory, figuring out the levels etc etc.

**Robert Carr's Mormonoids
From the Deep**

### Exploration Games:
### Myst, Hysterectomy, etc

These are another way to lose a lot of time out of your life. Why aren't you out hacking something?

### Weird or X-Rated Games:
### Mormonoids From
### the Deep, etc

A game like this offers unique opportunities for learning. Go for it.

### Slacker Computer Games:
### Solitaire, Hearts, etc

Get a life. Get a modem. Get some new friends. Drink more Brainwash. No shuriken for you.

## Part 2: Offline Games

*"Wish I Was Like You—Easily Amused."*

If you don't do dumb drugs, if you cultivate your haqr smarts, doors slam shut all over the world. Gablammal-lallammmm. You are on the outside looking in at large chunks of your culture. Low thresholds for amusement, aided by chemicals, is the rule in public merriment. Given enough chemical support, anything's bearable, and some things tip over into being enjoyable—like watching a man hitch his pants repeatedly and stare at another man for several minutes—yes, there may be a correlation between the long decline of baseball and the decline in alcohol consumption. If you demand that things be intrinsically interesting, your opportunities for public fun go right down the tubes. You can take the anthropologist approach, and learn to enjoy your culture secondhand. Is it melancholy fun, observing your parents or friends as they watch sitcoms on TV? Is it worse when you take notes? Discuss.

You're not alone. In real life, offline, there are others shuffling around outside the gates of popular culture, and not all of them are homeless. If you're lucky, some of them will be nerds and cyberpunks, and you can all start up a card game.

## Magic

Magic is good training for the Next Cold War. In this game you pit your card deck against your enemies' decks. Usually, the more $$ your cards cost, the more Magic you have, and

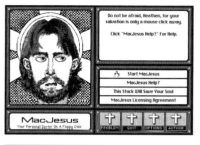

**Robert Carr's MacJesus**

the easier you win. The long-term strategy in both Magic and a Cold War is the same—buy more expensive armaments. You will have ever-neater toys, and you will simultaneously SPEND YOUR ENEMIES TO DEATH. Huh uh huh uh. One-half shuriken.

## Hacker

This is a fun game from Steve Jackson Games of Austin, Texas. Any offline game keeps you away from the real thing, but Hacker may spark the haqr urge in your younger sisters and brothers and cousins and the kids you babysit for. Come on, corrupt the youth—do your bit for the future. Three shuriken.

## The Glass Bead Game

This game doesn't really exist yet, although some nerdz are playing 2-D versions of it. It's a highly intellectual thing that maps associations of one card to others in a pattern, and when you add a card you have to explain how your card fits the pattern. It takes a lot of smarts. Maybe it makes you smarter or maybe it keeps you that way. Smarter is always okay. Two propeller beanies.

## Dungeons, Dragons, Duh

This game may be used as a first step when you're out to convince your family that there's a life beyond TV. It can lead them gradually to playing Hacker, and then... and then... One shuriken, to start.

# Chapter 16
# Cyberpunk
# Lifestyle Hints
*Trends, Faves and Hates*

## Interior Decorating Tips and Stylin Furnishings

If you live in institutional housing—e.g. in a dorm or with your parents—you may have to be cool about this. Furnishing your personal space to look like an abandoned factory may not be hackable. If you're lucky enough to live in an abandoned factory you don't need to worry about furnishings at all. Just skip forward to the next section.

If you're trying for **deep geek**hood, make it look like you're a working hacker by arranging stacks of manuals, old hardware, eviscerated PCs and reams of printouts. Don't throw out your Jolt cans—use them as decorator accents! Print out old Internet **RFC**s and sleep on them to give them a patina. Glue a giant sheet of 1/8″ tileboard to one wall and scribble mysteriously on it with whiteboard markers.

*Cybertip: A gutted VAX 11/780 acts as a conversation focus... and it's almost a giveaway at most university auctions.*

### Amusing Potted Plants

Chia Pets are odd-shaped ceramic pots that grow green hair if you remember to water them. Any sort of Chia Pet shows you have a sense of whimsy, but Chia Don King or Chia Hitler are a real **win**. Carnivorous plants are good, but you can kill them if you aren't careful, just like Chias, or children, or cats. If you have these things you've gotta check on them every month or so... toss 'em some meat... water or maybe exercise them.

### Stickers, Posters and Logos

Be strategic about this. Do you really need that Asian cutie on the ceiling above your bed? Any **IRL** Asian cuties who you lure into your space may bolt right out again before you can engage them in a meaningful conversation. Do you really *mean* that poster with the skull and worms on your door? Will it generate more scorn than fear? Think!

### What to Put on Top of Your Computer Monitor and Why

Don't put anything on top of your monitor that is flammable or likely to leak or explode. Next.

### Nerd Comic Strips

*Dilbert* is cool. It's written and drawn by an actual nerd, Scott Adams, who sometimes uses real technical terms. *Too Much Coffee Man* is very cool, too. *TMCM's*

drawn and written by Shannon Wheeler, a nerd from
Austin, Texas. Lots of cool people are from Austin, Texas.
Forget *Spiderman, Batman,* and *[Anyotherprefix]man.*

## The Haqr Basic Diet, Stunt Foods and Intimidating Soft Drinks

Ramen with Tabasco Sauce is a way of life. Anything else is just for fun. For example, get festive when unexpected guests drop by your factory—compress a loaf of vitamin-enriched whitebread into a ball, slice and serve. Jolt cola is another staff of life. Jolt's a smart drug, naturally rich in caffeine. But for special occasions, the ultimate softdrink has to be navy-blue Brainwash. Read the label. You'll notice many misspelled Chinese herbs, two kinds of chili peppers, and other powerful yet legal ingredients that just won't leave you be. You'll pace, rant, stay up all night. The Skeleteens make other brain-slamming softdrinks, but Brainwash is the mightiest. We don't know the Skeleteens, and we hope never to meet them. They are probably very scary.

*Cybertip: This is not a product placement, nimrod. In fact, after several Brainwashes, we're ready to kick your âz for even thinking that.*

## Music That Doesn't Suck

This is a huge and ever-expanding category. Nerds at this moment still like King Missile, the Ramones, Mortal Coil, Frank Black and Spot 1019, but if yr cyber enough, you can listen to anything you finking want.

## Squeaky/Cuddly Toys
## With Really Good Rationalizations

You can roll around in this stuff, however fluffy, twee or nelly it may be, if you're prepared to fight for it. Wit, extreme cool, or superior mus-

cle will bring you **winnage** here... and now that we thnk about it, everywhere else. Wit, extreme cool, and superior muscle is the primate system for getting or keeping anything you phorquing WANT. What a horrible thought. It's not a pretty planet.

## Rubik's Hypercubes or Rubik's Dodecahedrons or Rubik's Other Strange Shapes and High-Tech Intellectual Adult Transformers in the Shape of Interlocked Rings, Chains, Blocks, Helices, and Platonic Solids That Shapeshift into other Configurations of Rings, Chains, etc etc but only if you do them exactly right, which is very difficult or impossible, but which gather dust, take lots of room on your monitor, and taunt and sneer at you every time you look at them

You do not need this kind of grief. Scroom. Stuff them all into a big water-repellent bag, even unto the last red-plastic facet and wire spring. Leave them on the doorstep of somebody who needs to lose several months.

# SECTION 5

## [ CYBERPUNK... THE INNER SCENE ]

# CHAPTER 17
# Cyberpunk Secrets Revealed!

*(Yes, Just as We Promised—Revealed!)*

**Why Cyberpunks Seldom Have Their Organs Pierced**

Piercings are good because they are permanent… this makes it easier to identify idiots. No, but seriously, think about it—do you want to do something to your body if there's no UNDO? That's what it means, *permanent*. Think! When they make up your dossier at Interpol, how will they deal with the last part of the description:

Identifying Marks—
Scars, Tattoos, Piercings, Brandings and Amputations

Will they be able to answer just YES YES YES YES YES YES? Think!

## The Real Reason Why Cyberpunks Need to Encrypt Their Email

Cyberpunks don't want anyone reading their email. Their email may be ordinary, it may be $T00P1D, it may be very *confidential*. No matter—NOBODY reads their email. Who reads yours?

## What Cyberpunks Are Doing at 3 AM in That Dumpster

Trashing. Keep your head down and hold that light lower, please.

## Why Cyberpunks Avoid Altered States

A cyberpunk's brain is nearly hir FIRST-favorite organ. Making this organ work better is a clear priority. Caffeine is a **smart drug**, and a cheap, easy and legal smart drug at that. Jolt, which is naturally rich in caffeine, never hurt anybody, and may have helped many a 'punk make it through the night… maybe. Even if smart drugs don't work, dumb drugs almost certainly DO, or who'd bother with them? Dumb drugs all work on the same principle: They disable your **haqr smarts**. Some dumb drugs make you feel like you're having more fun than the situation really warrants. Some make you more confident than you should be. Some make you more violent than you'd better be, and some of them KILL BRAIN CELLS— they're neurotoxins—like alcohol…

## Coping With Neurotoxins

The true cyberpunk will only occasionally stoop to cloud hir sensorium. When that occasion arises— maybe at a **Con**—the cloud of choice is supposed to be beer. Cons favor beer because it's cheap, ugly, desper-

ate, and promiscuously available. YOU, on the other hand, favor beer because of its conspicuous consumption. You can sit there and swill beer after beer all night, burping and mopping your mouth with your leather sleeve. WHAT???

Yes... you CAN do this, without your neurons squeaking in fear. We will now tell you the secret that inner cyber persons have long known. The way to hold your alcohol is in your hand. Festively. You gesture with it, point with it, press it to your brow. One beer will serve you all night if you're on a tight budget. If there's a host bar, or other people are buying, you can guzzle beer after beer, one obnoxious loud SIP—teensy sip—per beer. Then you somehow...

forget about this beer. Losing your beer on crowded surfaces is usual. Accidentally elbowing—or better still—kicking your beer off things and hollering rowdily for a replacement is a better move. Popping the new top with maximum hoop-la, then staggering to the bathroom to tip it untasted down-toilet is really optimal. The point is to shine cool and intellectually unscathed at 3 AM when the fools around you are drowning. This is the time when you can taunt your enemies mercilessly. They won't remember a thing. Stand back and watch them self-destruct.

*Cybertip: Helping your enemies destroy their credibility with neurotoxins is a major reason to show up at Cons.*

## Why Some Cyberpunks Love *Star Trek* Even Though It Sucks, When Cyberpunks Always Diss What is Lame and Useless

The secret is that *Star Trek*, in all its generations and spinoffs, was designed to be *habit-forming*. *Star Trek* is the first virtual designer drug. Like the cousins of opium, a *Star Trek* episode induces a pleasurable buzz for a programmed length of time. Like the opiates, it does so by raising your gullibility levels and jamming your critical faculties, thus lowering your pleasure threshold. You have more fun when most of your wits are AWOL. This experience is repeatable, and after a while it NEEDS to be repeated, or withdrawal begins. The true nature of *Star Trek* has never been divulged by its creators, because Gene Roddenberry had them all Taken Care Of. If you don't believe this, watch a *Star Trek* junkie happily ingest a cheesy early Gen-1 episode for the 19th or 20th time. Are you suspicious yet?

**What Cyberpunks Actually Admire, and Why**.
Cyberpunks admire ingenuity. Wilyness. Gutz. These qualities make up **haqr smarts**. Cyberpunks admire courage in weird situations. Most of all, they admire a **good hack**. A good hack can be abstract, like a new programming approach, a new algorithm, an unexpected solution to a problem—or it can be utterly physical, like Instant Suit.

The Instant Suit hack involves a dark-gray suit front with a white shirt and black tie sewn into it, with velcro around the neck to hold it in place. You drape it over your 2600 t-shirt while your co-conspirators take your polaroid for your fake Security-Pass photo. Add a couple of fake numbers, laminate it, and there you are, looking official—you're an Instant Suit.

A good hack is… well, a very phamous ex-haqr once said, "You wanna know what a good hack is? See that lamp on the wall over there? A good hack would be if I could figure out some way, using that lamp, to get myself a beer."

**Secret Cyberpunk Handshaking,
Signals and Head Motions**
I'm really sorry about this. I had them all written out, complete to the last twitch and shout, but at the last moment I got some email that made death threats feel like a footmassage. Sorry. You'll have to figure this stuff for yourself. I can tell you, though, that you must never, never under any circumstances lean over and make like you're sniffing at a cyberpunk's leather jacket, or… Okay, that's all I can say.

# Chapter 18
# Cyberpunk:
# The Inner Game

## The Tao of Punk; The Secret Dancing Masters of Cyber; and Everything You Wanted to Know About Cyber but Were Too Lame to Ask

Now we have to break the news to you. It's our painful duty to divulge that anyone calling hirself a cyberpunk is a lamer—by definition. If you sign on #hack with a cyber-anything handle you'll be booted off instantly. The term is a torturous embarassment to real haquers, freekers and culture pirates. They and their outlaw or underground activities are never to be tainted with what they call the C word. If you secretly identify with Cyberpunk, this word falls out of your vocabulary RIGHT NOW. If someone calls you a cyberpunk you sneer horribly and say something offensive. When you're next alone you can high-five yrself.

## The Hidden Hierarchy of Cyberpunk Revealed, From Bottom to Top.

Ideally, the cyberpunk wants to destroy hierarchies. Yeah right, but if you want to be a practitioner you gotta face facts in front. There are LEVELS of cyber, and these levels are based on expertise as well as Attitude. These levels will now be explained in horrible detail.

**wannabe**: Owns a Leather Jacket, Mirrorshades & Boots. Knows about Wm Gibson and Bruce Sterling (they're cool). Dad's getting a modem. Has heard of UNIX.

**newbie**: May or may not have kelly-green dreads. Dad has an account on America OnLine. Knows Netscape. Intends to buy a UNIX manual. Has read *Neuromancer* on paper, and bits of *The Hacker Crackdown* online. Knows some fone numbers that do cool stuff. Hangs at local BBSes. When people of this class go to **Con**s they get sneered at. Unless they're female, in which case their technical skills may get rapidly upgraded. There can NEVER be TOO MANY female cyberpunks.

**netcrawler/web-runner (cyber-yup)**: May have signed copies of *Neuromancer, Crystal Express, Burning Chrome, Snow Crash* and *Schismatrix* archived anaerobically, wanders Net freely, but seldom crosses over to wildside. Writes complete sentences with standard spelling. Knows practical UNIX for getting around comfortably. Signon name is respectable, maybe based on real name. May spawn a skanky pseudonym—a handle—for *night*crawling.

**dood**: Spells things like HAQR and D00D. Keeps a cookbook for doing weird stuff with telephones or UNIX. May go to 2600 meetings the first Friday of every month to update cookbook. Knows somebody who writes for *Computer underground Digest.* Has online visibility in hip d00d hangouts. May have evil handle featuring death, blood, insufficient light, slime, or heraldry.

**3L1T3 (lamer spelling of elite)**: The highest level you can reach, according to newbies and lamers, who may sneer at the 3L1T3 from sour grapes. The 3L1T3 are reputed to mumble UNIX commands in their sleep. They're believed to have a printout of William Gibson's TRW credit history—framed—above their monitors, and an encrypted file with Bruce Sterling's American Express Card number AND expiration date. The 3L1T3 were written about in *The Hacker Crackdown* and *Wired.*

**eleet, 31337 or 'l33t (dood spelling of elite)**: The eleet go to 2600 meetings only to teach. Members of the true elite may be visible, and known to be eleet or EL1T3, but it's best for them to stay invisible, and remain only…

**elite**: The secret masters. They've rewritten a UNIX kernel. They have Bruce Sterling's PGP passphrase and the key to Gibson's back door. The elite were NOT mentioned in *The Hacker Crackdown* and *Wired* never heard of them. The elite hang out only in fully-encrypted IRCs and invite-only loops. What, you're out of the loops? Eat your heart out.

**pica**: Just forget it. This level is so far BEYOND elite that even if I could explain it, you'd never understand. Try checking back in *Cyberpunk Handbook Upgrade,* due out in 1999.

# Chapter 19
# The Parental-Discretion
# Special: Sects and
# Politics... and Recipes

*In fact, you might want to tear this section out before your children get ahold of it, and save it until they turn 35*

---

**Disclaimer:**

I hereby declare that I am (greater than or equal to) twenty-one years of age and my interest—no, better to say, my faint *curiosity* about the basic stuff of primate life—s*x, religion, politics, and cookery—is completely detached and nothing like purulent.  I promise I will remain unscathed by insights revealed herein, and that I will forget everything I read, immediately.

In the event that I become a Satanist and kill myself in a devil-rite I will not blame Random House, and I forbid my estate to sue, threaten or spam Random House on my behalf.

**Signed, Sincerely**

**Name** _____

**Date** _____

---

# Part 1: The Joy of Sects

Cyberpunks are just like anyone else, only more so. It follows that cyberpunks are not blind to any aspects of mind, including those called spiritual. Do you assume that cynical, technology-worshipping, leather-wearing persons don't bother about these things? Well, you're wrong. Agnosticism, while consistent with the lifestyle, is nowhere required. You can keep on practicing the religion of your choice, or the religion of your parents or your ethnic group, while being a cyberpunk, no problem.

However, cyberpunks display some cultural diversity, and in your investigations of cyberpunk lifestyles you may encounter some unusual religious practices. Do not be alarmed. Rational behavior is expected from cyberpunks in public. You will likely not be forcibly converted to anything. Just smile and say no thank you.

## Church of the SubGenius

This started as an outrageous parody of organized religion, but as organized religion has become equally outrageous, SubGenius has had to retrench as a branch of the Irony movement. SubGenius people tend to worship Irony in its more accessible aspects. Some highlights of the cult are:

1. The grinning pipe-smoking deity Bob Dobbs

2. The Hero's Quest—the search for Slack, which is the most valuable element in the universe

3. Ivan Stang, who doesn't exist

We may be up for the SubGenius hit-squad for divulging this, but Ivan Stang is just a title that gets passed around among the SubGenius Inner Illuminati. Be warned. If any authors of this book end up hanged under a bridge so that the tide washes them, those of us who are left will infallibly pin it on this year's Ivan Stang.

### Santería, Vodoun, Condomblé (Hoodoo)

Popularized by William Gibson in *Mona Lisa Overdrive*—or was it that other one?—Vodoun is still rather hip. There's a whole delicatessen tray of godz, and if you find any of them congenial, you can pick that one to be owned by. You get its sign tattooed on your ankle, and you allow it to take over your body now and then, granting you most of the advantages of multiple personality without the liabilities. Foremost for cyberpunk cachet is Legba, God of Crossroads Actual and Metaphorical. Legba has dominion over the Net and the Web. He presides over Digital Signal Processing in general. Legba manages encryption and decryption, fonephreaking, computer intrusion, the Ways and Means Committee, and all World Premieres. Vodoun expressively synthesizes the intellectual and the artistic. Finding a local congregation may be a problem in most areas.

### Rastafari

This religion is organic, and very very Green. (see **Politics**) A Rasta's life is devoted to *vegetables*—eating them, smoking them and then imitating them—*and the letter "I"*.

## Secular Buddhism

There are two important branches of Buddhism in this country: Zen and Vajrayana. Zen is minimalist and intellectual, very black-on-black. Vajrayana has recently boiled over from Tibet, frothing with magick and crazy wisdom, colorful flags and cool festivals. Cool.

Lots of cyberpunks call themselves buddhists. Some are... and some aren't. For decades it's been hip to call yourself a buddhist. And it's not a demanding sort of thing—you can eat animals, drive cars, grow your hair, fire guns, or do anything else you really want to do, and call yourself a buddhist. After all, who's going to ask to see your buddhist card?

If you really *are* a buddhist, you may stand some chance of becoming Enlightened. From descriptions, we infer that getting Enlightened is something like growing up, but we're skeptical.

## Cyber-Hinduism

This old fave has been appropriated by a sector of hackery, who've adapted it to serve their special needs. Bug extermination, just for starts. Many a haqr hard drive reeks of plum incense. Many a monitor supports a squat chubby dude with an elephant head—Ganesh, or Ganesha. Ganesh is the remover of obstacles. Does that suggest anything to you? Here's a computer intruder mantra:

Ganesh... Stomper of roadblocks... Ganesh ... Scarfer of passwords... Ganesh... Crusher of firewalls... Ganesh... Root of the system... Root ... Root ... Root ... Root ... Ganesh!

## CyberPancretism (Zippies)

Imagine the works of Aleister Crowley (pronounced like Crow, not crowd), Genesis P. Orridge, Herman Trismagistus, and the guy who wrote the Cthulhu stories all folded in with the other sects mentioned in this section, then mixed up to a froth—and that is the Order of the New Dawn, or the Order of the Temple of Ough, or the Other New Ordnung. People who take up this stuff can expect major lifestyle changes. Ceremonial daggers. Smart-delicatessen. Obligatory Rave attendance.

## Folie à Deux
## (Dyadic Black Hole, Twisted Pair)

This is a do-it-yourselves thing that you and your loved one generate between you. As your relationship develops, intuition and empathy grow, until it seems that you are responding telepathically to each other's subtlest thoughts… and from then on, many transcendent things can happen, yes. Depending on the chemistry between you, you might achieve a psychosis built for two. You may become convinced of dubious things. That you have made contact with other planets. That you know who killed Kennedy. That you understand the meaning of life, or *Thus Spake Zarathustra*. Or that you both (each in your own way) have become possessed by Kurt Cobain. At this point you should go into couple counseling immediately.

## Devil Worship and the Faustian Pact

A cyberpunk longs for knowledge, and knowledge is power, so… So *what?* If you've even thought about cutting a deal with Satan, I'll bet you fought UNIX and lost. Ye of little brain, don't mess with this either. Over the centuries, results have been less than mixed.  Also, we're told that having to be exorcised is worse than going to a Fat Farm.  Follow these maxims scrupulously:

1. Don't make overtures to supernatural powers.

2. Be suspicious of any lawyer who agrees to handle your case, and

3. Certainly don't try to go it alone with *Do Your Own Faustian Pact: Negotiating a Win-Win Contract With the Sales-Rep of Darkness*, $14.95 from Volo Press.

You've been warned.

## Part 2:  Politics

### Anarchists
You remember that big

that Beavis and Butthead painted on Mr. Anderson's house?  It stands for Anarchy, dude.

*Sure it does.*

Kropotkin—a serious Russian 19th century Anarchist political philosopher—would weep.

It stands for AnarchISM, which isn't, like, chaos—it's a *system*. Over the last couple of centuries there have been many organized (!) Anarchist movements. And much high-level debate about how to achieve the utopian dream—human societies which can maintain themselves free from the oppression of government.

The debate continues. Nowadays we've got:

> 1. The Crypto-Anarchists, who are hoping to overthrow everything by encrypting their email
>
> 2. A new wave of Wobblies (Industrial Workers of the World), who used to be Syndicalist-Anarchists but now are Communo-Anarchists, and who usually work as industrial music djs on pirate radio
>
> 3. Still with us are the Individualist-Anarchists, who refuse to join anything, led by Max Stirner, who is still dead—that guy online is somebody else.
>
> 4. The so-called Anarchists Without Adjectives, who are now, and always have been… ineffable.

Throughout their history, Anarchists of all stripes have hoped to build a better world through the free exchange of ideas—or insults and one-liners—and a praxis based on a kind of planned spontaneity…        *BORING!*

Cyberpunks are usually closer to the Beavis and Butthead version, only Beavis stops the frog baseball every so often to quote Guy Debord, or the Situationists. "Hey… heh… he said 'Politics of *Desire*"!!! Heh heh. Heh."

## Greens

Eco-freaks with computers? Believe it or don't, many cyberpunks are Green. How and why do they manage it—to hate the Grid, but love the Net? Maybe they feel guilty for putting together the telerobotic systems that incinerated Iraq. Or maybe they like settling down with a nice complex problem—like how to make computers run by photosynthesis. Or how to take a meadow full of hypersensitive touchy-feely freaks—each one of whose opinions were formed by direct psychic contact with the original high priestess of Atlantis—and help them reach consensus. Or how to build a Gaia-loving low-cost hay-bale house when hay is so expensive. Or, how to have social justice and a clean environment in a technical society without coercion. Now people... *play nice.*

## Libertarians

More than 50% of cyberpunks claim to be some shade of Libertarian. Libertarianism is—yes—the trendiest political category in the western world right now, running neck-and-neck with fascism, which would appear to be its opposite. Actually the two seem to be fraternizing okay in most countries, maybe synthesizing together a kind of Magna Carta for white guys.

Cyberpunk Libertarians, on the other hand, are not synthesizing with anybody. They oppose any form of censorship, and favor legalizing drugs, prostitution and all amino acids. They want to end taxes, dismantle the federal government. And defend to the death their Second Amendment right to stockpile their own household nukes and bio-weapons. *They can take my cold-fusion rocket-launcher when they pry it from my cold radioactive hand.*

R. U. Sirius says: *To understand the probable outcome of the Libertarian vision, see any cyberpunk B movie wherein thousands of diseased, desperate and starving families sit around on ratty old couches on the streets watching television while rich megalomaniacs appropriate their body parts for their personal physical immortality. Hmmm, sound familiar?*

## Dystrophians

Nah—we can call them by their real name—Extropians. Extropians! Extropians are a small and powerless minority and we can taunt them at will. Extropians are the Futurist people who want to build mini-machines to build micro-machines, which will then build nano-machines, which will go in and brush out your arteries like a street sweeper. Rumor has it that Extropians also want to freeze their heads after uploading their personalities into the Net. Is the whole Web trembling at the thought?

## Ultra-Leftists

Nostalgia politics. While Libertarianism is very nineties, a remnant of cyberpunks are ultra-leftists, yearning for that good-time feeling of the late 1960's— back when the Weathermen, the Black Panthers and the Yippies were going to overthrow greedy capitalism and its government puppets by "picking up the gun" and "offing the pig"… on acid.

## Conspiratists

Some cyberpunks are into Conspiracy Theory. This is a new category for politics, but it fits the criteria. Really, the single most important concern of politics—who is doing what to skew up your chances for a future?—is exactly what conspiratism is about. We're talking about *survival*. When paranoia is important to you, the usual suspects are:

1. Paramilitary branches of organized religions (Opus Dei, Hadassah, the Danites)

2. Organizations set up to counter them (P-2, the Masons, the Rotarians)

3. All governments, and some of their sub-agencies

And if you like worrying about things, some long-term conspiracy faves are:

1. Why various Kennedys are dead

2. Which public figures are being impersonated by gray aliens

4. Who's behind all the extra-low-frequency irradiation of food and people

5. Mind control—orbital lasers? Or intranasal implants?

7. How to attract UFO abduction by aliens (gray or of color)

There are some ongoing minor concerns, such as who killed Pope John XXIII, who's doing routine maintenance on the ozone-eating machines in the Brazilian rain forest, the REAL reason why Bill Clinton backs the Clipper Chip. And what the Global Business Network really *wants*.

## Part 3: S*x

We intend to pull no punches here. This section is about s*x. We aim to talk about this sort of thing openly and in a candid, even Scandinavian, fashion. This should not be offensive, because cyberpunks disdain the ordinary in favor of the exotic and the less strenuous. Nowadays the usual sort of thing is not only risky but truly dangerous, what with plagues and nondisclosure agreements. Cyberpunks, always inventive, have discovered other ways for coping with... you know.

### SM (SanoMasochism)

Tying your accomplice up and whacking hirm with a cat-o-nine-tails is much easier and safer than s*x. Moreover, in a s*x-negative society, it is much *nicer* than having s*x. All in all, in this country in this decade, SM beats doing things with one's janitols.

### Tantra

This is much more work than having s*x. In fact, it's like having s*x while juggling plates. Tantra takes concentrated religious focus, a loving commitment, and months of practice with a personal trainer. If you want to find books about Tantra, go to the Religion section in the library and peer through the glass into the locked case.

### Fetishes

If you really REALLY like shoes or latex, the world is

much better now. In olden times you had to fantasize, hope, and maybe pay dearly for your hidden (snuffle) *desires*. Nowadays the average birthday party gives you more latex, tattoos, and spike shoes than you're likely to be comfortable with. It's one-stop shopping, too—sing that body eclectic—because piercings, shavings, leather fringe and thumbscrew earrings might appear on the SAME PERSON, with fangs on top. This is the life.

### Bestiality
We're not sure about this category. We've heard some things, that's all. Bugs Bunny, Herro Kitty. That lioness in *The Lion King*—well, any animal by Disney. King Kong. Gojiro. Sonic the Hedgehog. …Barney?

# Part 4: Advanced Cyberpunk Cookery
The key to this cuisine is *haqr mind in the kitchen*. Innovation! Courage! Cunning! Here are some proven recipes for quick, delicious, festive meals demonstrating the spirit of cyberpunk.

### Cyber
On the cyber side, here's a nearly instant dinner that is rapturously seductively, corruptingly delicious, although StJude originally designed it merely as a thought experiment. Nobody—as far as she knows—has ever used gorgonzola as a cooking oil. Until now.

Slice a couple of Belgian endives longwise and steam the slices until their stems can be easily pierced by a fork. Put them in a strainer, shake them gently and set them aside to drain. Put a big frying pan over a medium flame. Hack a great whacking chunk—maybe a quarter-pound—of american gorgonzola into small chunks. Throw the cheese into the hot pan, stir it around. The cheese will separate instantly into golden oil and vile crufty scum. You can skim the scum, which will make the dish look better and taste less intense. If you're that sort of person. When the gorgonzola sizzles, add the endive slices and turn the heat all the way up. Fry the slices in the cheese until their surfaces become a little crispy. While they're frying in the open pan, drop half a pound of fresh squid-ink pasta into boiling water. Drain the pasta when it's al dente and toss it energetically in a serving bowl with the juice of one lime and a cup of bruised (rolled on a board until they pop slightly) blueberries. Picture it: slick grey pasta with purple streaks and blue-black beads. Scummy gold-green endive.

Orgiastic. Serves two.

## Punk

If you don't know endive, couldn't bruise a blueberry, and don't want to think about squid ink… relax. It's okay. When cyber fails… there's always punk. When special people drop by your factory, here's a festive advanced recipe—also StJude's creation—that rivals punk culture's best.

Slice all the way around the wrapping of a freshly-purchased loaf of Wonderbread, and lift off the whole top, leaving the bread standing in the bottom half of its wrapper. Fan the tops of the slices so they stand slightly patulous. Open a jar of Cheez Whiz (Original Flavor) and drizzle it directly into the splayed loaf from end to end, sparing the outside of the heels. Grasping the heels at either end, compress the loaf into a firm ball the size of your dog's brain. Mold it into a smooth globe, healing the surface if necessary with a little water. Slice and serve at once, with pickle relish on the side.

Innovative, yet authentic. Serves two to ten.

## Vegan Punk

We're not sure if vegan punks will eat Wonderbread… maybe it's got something organic in it. Vegans live on pure stuff like tempeh, made of nothing but starch and fungus. They certainly do not eat things which involve cows, chickens, fish or bees. The really pure starchetarians may get brain problems if they don't take in enough amino acids. They get half-a-quart low on neurotransmitters and they could easily get caught in a vicious circle, trying to self-medicate their deficits by eating ever purer stuff. Vegan cyberpunks have no neurons to spare.

You can give your vegan friends' brains an infusion of aminos with this festive dish.

Carve tofu into some inoffensive shape, perhaps a tree. Bake at 450°, basting the branches with tahini, until firm and golden. Serve with a gravy of melted Hemprella™ cheese, made from pure denatured hemp.

For a more casual luncheon, the ingenious Tresca@aol.com suggests Vegan Pigs-In-Blankets. Whomp up a down-home mess of tofu dogs and hemprella wrapped in mochi (pounded rice flour + water). Brown quickly under a high flame or they'll melt down to a white, beige and yellow ooze.

# SECTION 6

[ CYBERPUNK... ARE YOU CYBER ENOUGH? ]

SECTION VI: CYBERPUNK... AI

ARE YOU CYBER ENOUGH?

# Chapter 20
# It's an Intelligence Test!

*Cyberpunk Skull-Tweakers and Fun Fare*

Cryptic crossword puzzles are hardcore. The hardest of the hardcore are British—Brits polish off cryptic crosswords that give Americans fits.

Try these. They're Brit-style, all-out, supercryptic, specialized-vocabulary, insider CYBERPUNK crosswords fit to cross your eyes. If you can solve even a few of the clues in each, you can probably pass for cyberpunk *right now*. Solve more than six or seven in each and we grant you a pass in this course. You are SUFFICIENTLY CYBER. You will be excused from the final exam.

If you solve everything in both puzzles we'll give you a special commendation and forcibly introduce you to Bruce Sterling.

# The All-Cyber Cryptic Crossword Puzzle

| | E | | K | | | | | 4 | | 5 | |
|---|---|---|---|---|---|---|---|---|---|---|---|
| C | Y | B | E | R | | 8 | 9 | 10 | | | |
| | E | | Y | | | 12 | | | | | |
| | | | | | | 13 | | | | | 14 |
| 15 16 | | | 17 | | | | | 18 19 | | | |
| 20 | | 21 | | | | | | 22 | | | |
| 23 | | | | 24 | | 25 | | | | | |
| | 26 27 | | | 28 | | 29 | | | | | |
| 30 | | | | | | 31 | | | | | |
| | N | S | A | | | 33 | | | | | |
| B | | | D | E | C | K | | | | | |
| U | | G | E | C | K | O | S | | I | C | E |
| G | H | O | S | T | | O | S | E | R | R | E |
| S | A | V | | O | | L | E | T | L | I | E |

## ACROSS

2. Hero of *Neuromancer,* short form. (2)

5. A certain ratio, promised in the wild blue yonder. (2)

6. and 8 across. This book you're holding is supposed to be about them. Think! (10)

11. What the Ramones said after they said gabba gabba. *You* might say this if you think this puzzle is unfair. Life isn't fair. (5)

12. What you are logically forbidden to name your mouse. (5)

13. A little nonsense I/O. (4)

15. Overflow on greater or equal, with all kinds of overt grief en route. (3)

17. Silly computer pranx, kidstuff. (4)

18. Nano nano. (3)

20. Across and 21. down. For keeping the eyes cool. (12)

22. A jewel for 6. and 8. across. (3)

23. Acronym for the Brotherhood of Erics, an ancient conspiracy. (2)

25. Count on this, loser! (4)

26. Female nerd sibling. (3)

28. Harassed 26. across. (5, 2)

30. An animal that plays fetch. (6)

31. What you gotta walk, without falling over. (5)

32. Never speak aloud. It used not to exist, but it nameless stays, always. (3)

33. And never say this either. (3)

34. The initials of a very famous writer who invented CP. Also, initials of a very famous CP saying. (2)

35. A cyberpunk's favorite instrument. 20 points off your score if you get this one wrong, dirty minded weenie. (4)

38. Extremely cool crawling on your monitor—claws and scales and flies. (6)

40. Stop cold or kill. (3)

42. Old-fashioned spook in the machine. (5)

44. This means the operating system messed up. An ugly thing to see at 3 AM. (5)

46. What you should do to your file just before your machine cra  (3)

47. What to do with sleeping governments? (3, 3)

## DOWN

1. New kind of phones for inner space. (3)
2. Unlocks your encrypted email. (3)
3. Encryption! (6)
4. A recovery program for darkside hackers, darq _ _ _ _. (4)
5. A sound of relief uttered by a wacko. (3)
6. Fave heavy metal. (6)
7. Someone who doesn't program very well. (5)
8. According to Douglas Adams, don't! (5)
9. The stellar system. (4)
10. What it is that is power. (9)
14. You just had lunch in-house with a government agent. (3, 2, 4)
16. At least twice better than only one of these novelists? (7)
19. Strange. (5)
21. See 20. across.
24. An online publication for, logically enough, those who want to hack or phreak. (6)
25. In every flame war, this is how each side views the otherz. (5)
27. Likewise, someone who's watching you and your friends from bottom to top. (3)
29. That proves it. (3)
34. Tiny parasites that bite programmers. The worst are called Heisen. (4)
36. The kind of plasm that a 42. across has. (4)
37. Logically, this is just a thousand times more than ool. (4)
38. Bill Clinton's email zipcode: whitehouse. _ _ _ . (3)
39. A 180° turn from north-northwest. (3)
40. Out in the Big Room, outside of cyberspace. (3)
41. Back in cyberspace, this is an upside-down meeting place. (3)
43. You might repeat this when taunting a 7. down. (2)
45. Horrible little pencil-neck blue-eyed alien. NOT the Pres of Microsoft. (2)

## Name That Nym!

We had a bunch of famous pseudonyms/handles for you to match up with their real meat identities and social security numbers, but we thought about that one more time, and…

Well, so instead you'll have to make do with…

# The 3-Letter Acronyms from H.E.C.K. Cryptic Crossword

## ACROSS

1. The ultimate acronym—what most acronyms are! (4!)

4. A band that will probably be forgotten in the few lousy weeks it takes for this book to make it to the shop. It does pseudocyber shtick and horrible splatter routines that spray the audience with fake gore. (4)

8. Our country in action, in counter-intelligent activities. (3)

10. There's no accounting for some offices... but not this one, generally. (3)

11. Oh and btw... (2)

12. Offline. (3)

13. and 17. Werner Erhard's instant wisdom: _ _  _ _, so what? (2, 2)

14. Internet Protocol Anything. (3)

16. Sorta like the real thing. As in ant, tsetse, city. (3)

17. See 13.

19. You lose. (2)

20. A place set up outside the law of all lands, maybe not permanently. (3)

21. Your private key for nondigital cash. (3)

23. The sound it makes when you appear at the other end of the wire! (3)

24. You can have this with eggs, spam, spam, spam and spam. (4)

26. and 29. Undo undo! (4)

27. The federal endtable of investigation. (3)

29. See 26

30. That is extremely amusing. (7)

31. The Office of Federal Astrologers. (4)

32. The public-key encryption scheme invented by these three persons now enshrined forever in this acronym. (3)

33. The public agency that just wants to hold your keys for you. (4)

36. Automated teller machines on other planets. (4)

37. Good luck making these guys give you more credit than you deserve. (3)

38. The last pulse your machine will ever have. (3)

39. Shave with Occam's Razor and you'll merit one of these. (4)

## DOWN

1. Telecommunications protocol/internet protocol… maybe. (5)

2. A computer language that you pronounce like Thpanish. (4)

3. A recovery organization for people who can't stop speaking in acronyms. (2)

5. The Neuromeister. (2)

6. and 36. A cry of dismay as expanded artificial intelligence rubs up against electrical engineering! (6)

7. Rolling on floor mouthing curses. Okay, that's another give-away. (5)

9. Your international recreational café. (3)

15. When you can get to it. (4)

16. How you happen to fall into the Net. (4)

18. Everyone knows it's not Kansas. (2)

19. It looks like world's only NINE-letter acronym, but it's a town in the midwest. (9)

20. An analog of *finger()*. (3)

22. So the count is Spanish this time! No acronyms here! (4)

23. The high school dance *you* never got to—so maybe you were soldering chips! (4)

25. This sort of MUD is oriented around objects. (3)

27. Find out information assembled behind your back, just fill out these forms… (5)

28. Not literally the Electronic Freedom Foundation. (3)

30. Rolling on stomach, moaning and puking. (5)

32. That little old teenage wormsmith. Also, the G-rated version of what you hear online if you ask about stuff you should have looked up. (3)

34. Certain as death? (3)

35. Spinach and wiener sandwich. Southwest something. Oh, just fill it in! (3)

36. See 6. down.

## Twisters and Max Headroom Memorial Rebuses

Okay, we were faking it about these things, too. Tough. This is part of your training, here—learning to face disappointment with awesome cool.

## Answers to Puzzling Questions

### The All-Cyber Cryptic Crossword Puzzle

No Twisters, no—GET OVER IT!  Tough up!  And continue on to the next section… because now we're going to put your toughness to the test. Because it's… BOTTOM LINE TIME.

## The 3-Letter Acronyms from H.E.C.K. Cryptic Crossword

```
[1]T  [2]L  [3]A   S   ■   [4]G  [5]W  [6]A  [7]R
[8]C   I   A   ■   [9]I  [10]G  A   O
[11]P  S   ■  [12]I  R   L   ■  [13]I  F
[14]I  P  [15]A  C   ■  [16]S   I   M
 P   ■  [17]S [18]O [19]Y   L       C
 ■  [20]T  A   Z  [21]P   I  [22]N   ■
[23]P  O   P      [24]S   P   A  [25]M
[26]R  E   ■  [27]F [28]E   I      [29]D   O
 O   ■  [30]R  O   F   L   M   A   O
 M      [31]O   I   F   A   ■
 ■  [32]R  S   A  [33]N [34]I [35]S   T
[36]E  T   M   S  [37]T   R   W   ■
[38]E  M   P   ■  [39]K   I   S   S
```

# Chapters 21, 22, and of course 23
# Bottom Line Time:
## *Making It or Faking It*

## Cyberpunk Review

Are you cyber enough yet? Do you think you're ready
to PASS?                                    Prove it!

## The Final Exam
### *It's Not True/False, We Don't Grade On The Curve, Stop Sniveling*

So, you've made it to the end of this handbook. So what?
Before you declare yourself a sheer cool cyberpunk and
go out into the world, real or virtual, and make an azole
of yourself, there are a few things you ought to know.
First of all, while you were lip-reading your way through
this book, cyberpunk stopped being hip. Yep. Too late.
Now it's hip to be a Republican with a navel piercing—
check out IBM, Gingrich, *Wired*, and the
Spielberg/Katzenberg/Geffen/Gates posse, The Dream-
works. The "suits" now have noserings, tattoos, Dockers
and Nikes. Is this the end of the world as we know it, or
just détournabout as fair play? In either case, now may
be a good time to give up.

Just kidding. In order to pass your Final Exam and become
a Cyberpunk Illuminatus, you have to do the following:

**Find the spoofed online accounts of the three authors of this book.**

*Hint: these accounts purport to be those of powerful political figures, and all three end in .gov.*

When you figure out which ones are actually us, just send the following note to our bogus accounts: "Hey, faq you, you pizza ship. This is a felonious death threat!" Sign, adding your real home address and phone number. You will receive a special prize.

Alternately, you can be credentialed as a cum laude graduate of the R. U. Sirius School for Fake Media Cyberpunks by writing an essay that contains all the following elements:

> 1. A witty and ambiguous dismissal of the cyberpunk subculture that will still allow you to circulate as a spokesperson for same.

> 2. Juxtaposed quotations from Nietzsche, McLuhan, any French guy, and Nancy Sinatra so as to illuminate the profound paralyses of the post-post-modern condition.

> 3. Advocacy of some form of awe-inspiring new technology with a smirking aside that it may have unimaginably horrible consequences for the vast majority of humans.

> 4. If you're a manly sort of male, a snide sexual innuendo to separate the wymyn from the grrrls. (The

wymyn are the ones who complain to the authori-
ties. The grrrls are the ones who laugh along with
you while kicking you in the 'nufs.)

5. A sentence that implies you have special insider
knowledge about a technology you really don't know
shemp about.

Mix well, press into a well-greased 2000 words and get
it into a clueless overseas publication for a dollar a
word and up.

If you succeed, R.U. will credential you as an authentic Fake Media Cyberpunk. The rewards are many, but
the hours are long and you will probably be forced to
talk again and again about Virtual Reality without
throwing up.

### The Official Cyberpunk Hipness Checklist
Just hold it right there, please. Yes, you—could you just
step over here out of the line? That's right. Thank you.

If you would just step back into this room please?
Good—be careful of the machines, they're very expensive. Thank you.

Now, if you will, please remove and explain each item of
your clothing as you take it off. Please think carefully
before you speak. You can place them on this counter,
that will be fine. Then, afterwards, please demonstrate
for us your *laser pointer*.

We will wait. Thank you.

## APPENDIX A: Cyberpunk Valorized

### Careers Under Deconstruction

Cyberpunk walks on the wild side, always. But back in the eighties, Cyberpunk got jumped in a dark gray area of academia and brutally co-opted. Since then people have written a lot of theses about it, but Cyberpunk isn't recognized as a separate discipline. Yet. This means you can't get your degree in Cyberpunk. Yet. But you can come close. Being a Cyberpunk Deconstructionist is major fun, and makes $$, and for that you only need a degree in Critical Theory.

### The Semiosis of Black Leather, Chrome, Mirrorshades and Modems

We included this section to **valorize** our book with Cyberpunk-Wannabe Academics and get us reviewed in Journalz. So, in this space we had a finely-argued deconstructive discourse on Black Leather, Chrome, and all that other shimp. But the publishers felt the discourse wasn't commercial grade. Fax 'em. Let's do a finely-argued DIAGRAM.

**[A] mirrorshades**:  The shell protecting the naked self as Eye, repelling the observing Other and simultaneously securing the Self's own armed gaze. The mirrored surface is a potent metaphor of armor, as in "I'm rubber, you're glue, everything bounces off me and sticks to you," and also precisely mirrors the counterposed Authority—i.e. the California Highway Patrol.

**[B] black leather jacket**: Signifier of the Nomadic agent, the self-marginalized hacker of a centralized institutional Truth. This garment is also a mirror of law-enforcement uniforms, although those of previous years, i.e. as a rearview mirror.

**[C] boots**: The signifier of the phallic nature of the foot. Thereby, the prosthesis of pedic aggression.

**[D] laser pointer**:  Most saliently itself a technological prosthesis of phallism, and by analogy an extension of the territorial "ambit"—literally the arm-reach of ownership or the long arm of the law, as in "I put my mark on this" or perhaps, "I put a spell on you." The marking of surfaces with a coruscating ruby light may moreover be read as a mediated apotropaic blood-marking, as in Dumézil's variations on a theme from Passover… but then again perhaps not.

**[E] chrome**:  A mirror of the mirror, iteratively. (As in, sometimes a shiny thing is only a shiny thing.)

# APPENDIX B: ASCII CHARTS

A map of the ASCII character set, giving both octal and hexadecimal equivalents of each character, to be referred to as needed:

| 000 nul | 001 soh | 002 stx | 003 etx | 004 eot | 005 enq | 006 ack | 007 bel |
|---|---|---|---|---|---|---|---|
| 010 bs | 011 ht | 012 nl | 013 vt | 014 np | 015 cr | 016 so | 017 si |
| 020 dle | 021 dc1 | 022 dc2 | 023 dc3 | 024 dc4 | 025 nak | 026 syn | 027 etb |
| 030 can | 031 em | 032 sub | 033 esc | 034 fs | 035 gs | 036 rs | 037 us |
| 040 sp | 041 ! | 042 " | 043 # | 044 $ | 045 % | 046 & | 047 ' |
| 050 ( | 051 ) | 052 * | 053 + | 054 , | 055 - | 056 . | 057 / |
| 060 0 | 061 1 | 062 2 | 063 3 | 064 4 | 065 5 | 066 6 | 067 7 |
| 070 8 | 071 9 | 072 : | 073 ; | 074 < | 075 = | 076 > | 077 ? |
| 100 @ | 101 A | 102 B | 103 C | 104 D | 105 E | 106 F | 107 G |
| 110 H | 111 I | 112 J | 113 K | 114 L | 115 M | 116 N | 117 O |
| 120 P | 121 Q | 122 R | 123 S | 124 T | 125 U | 126 U | 127 W |
| 130 X | 131 Y | 132 Z | 133 [ | 134 \ | 135 ] | 136 ^ | 137 _ |
| 140 ` | 141 a | 142 b | 143 c | 144 d | 145 e | 146 f | 147 g |
| 150 h | 151 i | 152 j | 153 k | 154 l | 155 m | 156 n | 157 o |
| 160 p | 161 q | 162 r | 163 s | 164 t | 165 u | 166 u | 167 w |
| 170 x | 171 y | 172 z | 173 { | 174 | | 175 } | 176 ~ | 177 del |

| 00 nul | 01 soh | 02 stx | 03 etx | 04 eot | 05 enq | 06 ack | 07 bel |
|---|---|---|---|---|---|---|---|
| 08 bs | 09 ht | 0a nl | 0b vt | 0c np | 0d cr | 0e so | 0f si |
| 10 dle | 11 dc1 | 12 dc2 | 13 dc3 | 14 dc4 | 15 nak | 16 syn | 17 etb |
| 18 can | 19 em | 1a sub | 1b esc | 1c fs | 1d gs | 1e rs | 1f us |
| 20 sp | 21 ! | 22 " | 23 # | 24 $ | 25 % | 26 & | 27 ' |
| 28 ( | 29 ) | 2a * | 2b + | 2c , | 2d - | 2e . | 2f / |
| 30 0 | 31 1 | 32 2 | 33 3 | 34 4 | 35 5 | 36 6 | 37 7 |
| 38 8 | 39 9 | 3a : | 3b ; | 3c < | 3d = | 3e > | 3f ? |
| 40 @ | 41 A | 42 B | 43 C | 44 D | 45 E | 46 F | 47 G |
| 48 H | 49 I | 4a J | 4b K | 4c L | 4d M | 4e N | 4f O |
| 50 P | 51 Q | 52 R | 53 S | 54 T | 55 U | 56 U | 57 W |
| 58 X | 59 Y | 5a Z | 5b [ | 5c \ | 5d ] | 5e ^ | 5f _ |
| 60 ` | 61 a | 62 b | 63 c | 64 d | 65 e | 66 f | 67 g |
| 68 h | 69 i | 6a j | 6b k | 6c l | 6d m | 6e n | 6f o |
| 70 p | 71 q | 72 r | 73 s | 74 t | 75 u | 76 u | 77 w |
| 78 x | 79 y | 7a z | 7b { | 7c | | 7d } | 7e ~ | 7f del |

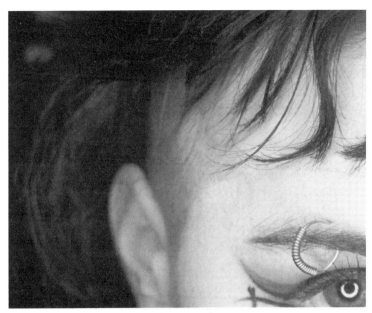

# Acknowledgments

The authors would like to thank the following groups and
individuals for their appearance in this book:
Eric Hughes and Tiffany L. Brown; our cover models.
The Otaku Patrol Group: Desmond Crisis, Belladonna, Todd
Barrett, London Nonstop, Christian Drägos, and Jade Gunnarson.
Thanks also to Heide Foley,
and Bart's dead cat Puff, who appears as himself.

For assistance in the production of this tome we'd also
like to thank, Karen Huff, Heide Foley, Kate Enochs,
and Desmond Crisis.

A special thanks to Susan Lawson

This book was designed and illustrated by Bart Nagel,
with additional illustrations by St. Jude.

# Portraits of the Artists:

```
#############
#  ///  \\\   #
#  // -00 (\   #
#  ((( - ))))  #
#  ))))\ /((((  #
#############
```

**Jude Milhon** is a vivacious, well-dressed female in apparent good health. She was born in Indiana, reared as a Marine Corps brat outside Washington, DC, lived in Cleveland and Manhatten for far too long, then visited Bay Area, California and stayed forever. She is an ex-UNIX programmer, a former political and Civil Rights activist, an ex-editor of MONDO 2000 magazine, and an ex-Physician Assistant licensed to do brain surgery under the laws of the State of California.

A cultural terrorist and polygamist, she lives in a little clearing near both of her "husbands", one of their "wives" and their two odd-parented "children," one of them grown up, in sleepy rural Berkeley, California.

She wrote the Irresponsible Journalism column for MONDO 2000, dealing out technology with humor, and invented the armed interview while working for that zine. She has already published several well-received haiku.

```
#############
#  /==$=\ )   #
#  // -00 (\   #
#  ((( - ))))  #
#  ))))\ /((((  #
#############
```

**R. U. Sirius** is co-founder of the legendary technoculture magazine MONDO 2000 as well as the co-author of MONDO 2000: A USER'S GUIDE TO THE NEW EDGE. He is a contributing writer for WIRED, FUTURE SEX, BOING BOING, MIGHT and io magazines. His media rock band, Mondo Vanilli, has been confusing record labels for several years. He plays himself in the films *Virtual Love* and *Twists of the Wire*, and has appeared (as himself) on The Ron Reagan Show, Donahue, and CBS Nightwatch. He has been called lots of different names in various publications and has been compared to Andy Warhol, Beavis and Butthead, Voltaire, Charles Manson, David Letterman, Timothy Leary, and Gomez Addams. He admires Christy Canyon, Sub-Commandante Marcos, and Salvador Dalí.

```
#############
#  ___        #
#  /_\        #
#  |00  ?    #
#  \< /·     #
# ===\v /====#
#############
```

**Bart Nagel** is a tall drink of water. Born in The Netherlands and raised in The West's Most Western Town; Scottsdale, Arizona, he transplanted to the Bay Area and threw his lot in with the MONDO 2000 crew; art directing both the magazine and the MONDO book: A USER'S GUIDE TO THE NEW EDGE, as well as writing a regular column for the magazine with no theme and little function. As a photographer and illustrator, he has created images for TIME, NEWSWEEK, THE RED HERRING, MIGHT, JUICE, BEER: THE MAGAZINE, THE NOSE, THE CITY, and MONDO 2000.

He currently resides in Emeryville, California where he is designing two books; SUBAMERICANA with writer Tiffany L. Brown, and THE RED HERRING GUIDE TO THE DIGITAL UNIVERSE. He continues to thwart his captions.

ASCII Portraits by St. Jude

---

*This brilliant collaboration is producing other works such as* **How to Mutate and Take Over the World**, *from Ballantine. Except that Bart didn't do anything on that one.*